J. Wendell Macleod

McGill-Queen's/Associated Medical Services Studies in the History of Medicine, Health, and Society

SERIES EDITORS: S.O. Freedman and J.T.H. Connor

Volumes in this series have financial support from Associated Medical Services, Inc. (AMS). Associated Medical Services Inc. was established in 1936 by Dr Jason Hannah as a pioneer prepaid not-for-profit health care organization in Ontario. With the advent of medicare, AMS became a charitable organization supporting innovations in academic medicine and health services, specifically the history of medicine and health care, as well as innovations in health professional education and bioethics.

J. Wendell Macleod

Saskatchewan's Red Dean

LOUIS HORLICK

McGILL-QUEEN'S UNIVERSITY PRESS
Montreal & Kingston • London • Ithaca

©McGill-Queen's University Press 2007

ISBN 978-0-7735-3231-1

Legal deposit second quarter 2007
Bibliothèque nationale du Québec

Printed in Canada on acid-free paper.

McGill-Queen's University Press acknowledges the support of the
Canada Council for the Arts for our publishing program. We also
acknowledge the financial support of the Government of Canada
through the Book Publishing Industry Development Program (BPIDP)
for our publishing activities.

Library and Archives Canada Cataloguing in Publication
Horlick, Louis

J. Wendell Macleod : Saskatchewan's Red Dean / Louis Horlick.
(McGill-Queen's/Associated Medical Services studies in the history
of medicine, health, and society; 29)

Includes bibliographical references and index.
ISBN 978-0-7735-3231-1

1. Macleod, J. Wendell, 1905-2001. 2. Medical education—
Saskatchewan—History. 3. Medical education—Canada—History. 4.
Social medicine—Canada—History. 5. University of Saskatchewan.
College of Medicine—Biography. 6. Deans (Education)—
Saskatchewan—Biography. I. Title. II. Series.

RA464.M255H67 2007   610.71'1712425   C2007-900516-0

This book was designed and typeset by studio oneonone in
Sabon 10/13.5

Contents

Acknowledgments

This book is the last in a triad dealing with the history of the University of Saskatchewan's College of Medicine and Royal University Hospital. The first two, *Medical College to Community Resource: Saskatchewan's Medical School, 1978–1998*, and *They Built Better Than They Knew: Saskatchewan's Royal University Hospital, 1955–1992*, both appeared under my name. The present volume is a biography of J. Wendell Macleod, the man who played a critical role in establishing both the new College of Medicine and the University Hospital. Macleod's role at the University of Saskatchewan constitutes the largest single part of the book, yet it was only ten years in a long and extraordinary life. The rest of the book puts that singular contribution in the larger perspective of his life and work in Canada and around the world.

Macleod kept a record of almost everyone he met, and he left behind sixty-three appointment books covering the period 1924 to 1995. In these are recorded the hundreds of people with whom he had some kind of contact or relationship over those seventy-one years. Names, addresses, and dates of encounter were invariably noted, and occasionally he added tidbits of personal information. He also left diaries covering a similar span: an early diary of his college years, 1923–25, seven five-year diaries covering 1948 to 1980, and single-year diaries covering 1942 to 1945 and 1981 to 1995. For this last period only the diary for 1991 is missing.

Macleod was a prolific diarist and letter-writer. There were periods, usually coinciding with meetings and holidays, when he wrote little for weeks, but the diaries are a treasure-trove nonetheless, for they reflect a century of events and comprise a social history of the twentieth century. Macleod's comments were brief and to the point, and he never spared himself, especially when it came to his perceived administrative inadequacies. Nor did he refrain from dealing with personal problems and failings. He was highly conscious of family events, anniversaries, birthdays, deaths, and other significant rites of passage, and often attached relevant newspaper clippings to the diary page. Like the great essayist Montaigne, he re-read his diaries in later years and added or corrected some of the notes; these addenda nearly always included a date.

I am indebted to Anne McDonald, who began work on a biography of Macleod nearly a decade ago. She carried out extensive interviews with him but was unable to continue the work. She graciously made some of her notes available to me and provided insights into Macleod's character that were very helpful to me in writing the introduction and afterword. Letters and interviews with family, friends, and acquaintances were another rich source of biographical information. His correspondents included Alice Cameron, his secretary in Saskatoon; Sheila Duff Waugh, his administrative assistant during the ACMC years; Jola Sise, his long-time friend and companion; J. Peter Macleod, his son, and Peter's wife, Margaret. Helen Mussallem contributed a store of letters written during the years Macleod spent in Haiti. William Feindel, head of neurosurgery in the early years of Macleod's deanship in Saskatoon, provided further information.

Documentation of Macleod's career in Saskatchewan was provided by the University of Saskatchewan Archives, and we especially thank the archivist Cheryl Avery for her help. The National Archives in Ottawa, where many of Macleod's papers are deposited, were also the source of an extensive interview with Macleod by A.M. "Sandy" Nicholson taped in February 1978. A minister in T.C. Douglas's cabinet, Nicholson played an important role in recruiting Macleod to Saskatchewan. Peter Macleod was a rich source of miscellaneous papers, clippings, and photos.

The author is indebted to Dr J. Stuart Houston, who read parts of early drafts, and to professors Richard Rempel of McMaster University and Michael Hayden of the University of Saskatchewan, and Donald Ward who read later drafts and made valuable suggestions. The author thanks Roger Martin and Maureen Garvie, who edited the final draft and shepherded the manuscript to publication.

The author acknowledges Dr William Albritton, Dean of Medicine at the University of Saskatchewan, and President Peter McKinnon for their unstinting encouragement and support of this project.

The author thanks the following for permission to use pictorial and print materials: National Archives of Canada, University of Saskatchewan Archives, University of Ottawa, the *Ottawa Citizen*, the *Montreal Gazette*, and the *Canadian Medical Association Journal*.

LOUIS HORLICK, MD
Saskatoon, Spring 2007

Abbreviations

AAMC Association of American Medical Colleges
ACMC Association of Canadian Medical Colleges
AMA American Medical Association
AUCC Association of Universities and Colleges of Canada
CCF Co-operative Commonwealth Federation
CCRC Centretown Community Resource Centre
CCSN Canadian Council of Schools of Nursing
CDA Canadian Dental Association
CFPC College of Family Physicians of Canada
CMA Canadian Medical Association
CNA Canadian Nurses Association
CP Communist Party
CPSS College of Physicians and Surgeons of Saskatchewan
DNHW Department of National Health and Welfare
FC Frontier College
FSB Family Service Board
IDRC International Development Research Centre
JCM J.C. Meakins
JWM J. Wendell Macleod
LCME Liaison Committee on Medical Education
LSR League for Social Reconstruction

Med-Chi Medical Chirurgical Society of Montreal
MRC Medical Research Council
NCCUC National Conference of Canadian Universities and Colleges
NHW National Health and Welfare (now Health and Welfare Canada)
OPD Outpatients Department
PMO Principal Medical Officer
PRC People's Republic of China
RCNH Royal Canadian Naval Hospital
RCPSC Royal College of Physicians and Surgeons of Canada
RUH Royal University Hospital
RVH Royal Victoria Hospital, or the Royal Vic
SCM Student Christian Movement
SMO Senior Medical Officer
SPM (Department of) Social and Preventive Medicine
UH University Hospital
WHO World Health Organization
WPT W. P. Thompson
WUSC World University Service Committee

J. Wendell Macleod

Introduction

An Extraordinary Life

————□————

WENDELL MACLEOD ENJOYED reminding people that the year of his birth coincided with the start of the Russo-Japanese War in 1905. His knowledge of this relatively obscure fact and its relation to his existence highlights a facet of his idiosyncratic approach to human experience. The date resonates as a milestone in history, for it marked the opening salvo in the almost ceaseless conflict that characterized the twentieth century. Macleod's fascination with contemporary events and his sensitivity to their impact on ordinary people began early and continued throughout the course of a life that mirrored the momentous events of the century.

His exposure to the poverty of those his father served as a Presbyterian pastor and his own religious beliefs led him naturally to the Social Gospel. This movement held that Christianity was a social religion concerned with the quality of human relations on earth. It was a call for people to find meaning in their lives by seeking to realize the Kingdom of God in the fabric of society. This belief led Macleod to consider becoming a medical missionary when he entered university. His views on the centrality of religion to the "good life" never changed; his commitment to medicine, medical education, and social justice, and his innovative approaches to them, were steadfast themes of his life.

Early in his medical career he recognized that poor people were sick in different ways from rich people and that they did not receive the same level or quality of care. Later he became aware of the enormous disparities in health care between the rich and poor countries of the world. He observed that this aspect of medicine was never presented formally or realistically in medical courses. With this awareness came a growing belief that medical education distanced students from their essential task – the provision of health care that encompassed not only symptoms and their treatment but an assessment of the social, economic, and political world in which patients lived. Macleod's journey led him down countless roads and byways. Sometimes he took the well-travelled way, but more often his chosen course led him into uncharted territory. He was a trailblazer, recognizing new directions in medical education and health care long before many of his colleagues.

Some found his iconoclasm exhilarating, even inspiring; others reacted with suspicion ranging from wariness to hostility. His actions often baffled his contemporaries, but in later years his contributions were recognized by the Order of Canada and four honorary degrees from Canadian universities.

For some, he was a visionary, for others, a hopeless idealist, even a dangerous subversive. His detractors were particularly vocal during the prolonged and rancorous controversy that preceded the introduction of a comprehensive medical insurance plan in Saskatchewan in 1962. For Macleod the legislation represented a logical step in the evolution of medicine. His opponents saw it as a plot by a socialist government to subjugate an independent profession. Macleod was not easily intimidated. During his tenure as dean of medicine in Saskatoon, he revolutionized not only the teaching of medicine but its application in the public domain. His ten years in Saskatchewan, more than any other period in his life, tested his beliefs.

His zeal for living was apparent in a long life that in the early years ranged from childhood vacations on his grandfather Brodie's farm to his medical education at McGill University and residency at Barnes Hospital in St Louis. It continued through his time as a young practitioner in Montreal, his association with Norman Bethune, his wartime experience as a naval officer in Halifax, and a stint in group practice at the Winnipeg Clinic. It culminated with his deanship at the University of

Saskatchewan and his subsequent term as executive director of the Association of Canadian Medical Colleges. He greeted each new chapter of his life with enthusiasm and curiosity: all experience, whether his own or that of others, carried the potential for learning and enrichment. To paraphrase Tennyson, he strove to be part of all that he met. Looking back over the more than nine decades of his life, we may say that in large measure he succeeded.

Chapter One

The Early Years, 1905–1934

———□———

WENDELL MACLEOD was the first of four sons born to the Reverend John B. Macleod and Helena Brodie Macleod in Kingsbury in the Eastern Townships of Quebec. Both John and Helena came from rural backgrounds: John was born and raised on Prince Edward Island, where Gaelic was the language spoken in the home, and Helena was raised on a farm near the Upper Lachine Road on the outskirts of Montreal.

John Macleod started out as a potato farmer and a schoolteacher before enrolling at McGill University in Montreal to study arts and theology. He took the gold medal in philosophy and went on to Glasgow for a further year of study. While in Scotland he made a trip to Skye to visit his father's birthplace, then returned home to follow two of his three brothers into the Presbyterian ministry.

Wendell Macleod was born on 2 March 1905. Robert followed in 1907, Kenneth in 1913, and Archie in 1915. As the children were growing up, the family lived in a series of parishes in small communities throughout eastern Ontario and Quebec. They were near enough to Ottawa in 1916 to see the glow in the sky that was the fire that destroyed the Houses of Parliament. It remained a vivid memory for Wendell Macleod, and it is noteworthy that his parents, recognizing the historic significance of the events, awakened their eleven-year-old son to witness it.[1]

Macleod admired his father, to whom he credited his own egalitarianism, his dedication, his religious beliefs, and his awareness of social

The young family Macleod – Helena Brodie Macleod,
John B. Macleod, Wendell (age 7), Robbie (age 5) and cousin
"Gwen" Brodie (age 7)

inequities. His younger brother, Robbie, recalled their father as a man
of learning, a gentle man, devout Christian and dedicated pastor beloved by his parishioners: "But his real love was philosophy, and ... although he was sure of his ground, he was always willing to concede that
the other fellow might have something to teach him."[2]

John Macleod gave his eldest son the affectionate nickname "Slow
John" because of his tendency to become fascinated by objects and
linger over them. Macleod's memory of himself as a boy attributes as
much influence to his mother as his father: "Like my mother, I was
timid, even after adolescence, and as inclined to agree in order to be
agreeable. To compensate, I am sure that sometimes I was obstinate and
chose roles that would help me believe I was brave and rugged."[3]

After ministering in several rural parishes, including Martintown, Ontario (a congregation founded by the Rev. John Bethune, Norman Bethune's great-great-grandfather), John Macleod moved his family to Winchester, south of Ottawa. There the boys enjoyed four years of small-town life and spent summer holidays on their grandfather Brodie's farm in Quebec.

In March 1918 John Macleod moved to Montreal to take up the position of visitor to Presbyterian (and later, United Church) patients or inmates in hospitals, retirement homes, and Bordeaux Prison. He took Wendell and Robbie with him to Montreal so that they could attend high school there; Helena and the two younger boys stayed on in Winchester. Until they could get a flat, father and sons roomed together in downtown Montreal, first in the Presbyterian College, until the army took it over, then Strathcona Hall opposite the McGill campus.

Soldiers were everywhere, and the war seemed very close. The Germans had launched their last major offensive and were once more threatening Paris, as they had in 1914. Each evening crowds filled the intersection of Peel Street and Rue Sainte-Catherine to look for updates on the *Montreal Star*'s bulletin boards. Christmas 1919 was marked for the boys by a visit to Bordeaux to distribute gifts to the inmates. At fourteen Wendell Macleod came to understand that prisoners were not always desperate criminals but were often simply unhappy, unfortunate men, not all that different from him.

Throughout high school and university, he heard the stories of his father's former parishioners and friends who came to the Montreal General or the Royal Victoria Hospital for examination or treatment. Some were relieved and jubilant, but others found themselves facing major stress or financial disaster as a result of hospital charges and professional fees. Macleod later lamented that this aspect of medicine was never realistically presented in medical courses, except by Dr A.H. Gordon at the Montreal General.

Moving to a new school towards the end of term must have been a frightening experience for a small-town boy handicapped in French and unstable in mathematics. But friendships saved the day for Macleod, the closest being with Allan Ross, another son of a Presbyterian minister, who became a lifelong friend. In 1921 the two boys spent a week at a missionary conference at Knowlton on Brome Lake in the Eastern Townships. There they met Canadian missionaries who had spent years in China or India. The experience may have influenced Macleod's later

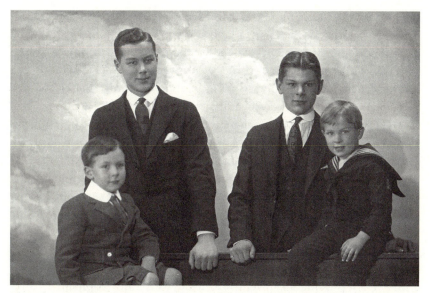

The "four musketeers": Ken (eight), Wendell (sixteen), Robbie (fourteen), and Archie (four), 1921

decision to take the eight-year combined science and medicine course at McGill with a view to serving in medical mission work.

The 1920s were a wonderful period for a university student in Montreal, and in his first two years Macleod enjoyed life to the full. He was eager to learn, enjoyed his classes, and quickly became involved in the social life of the university. He joined a fraternity and made many friends. Summers were pleasant too; his diary for 1924–25 lists the parties and social events he attended in and around the Island of Montreal. At this time he developed the lifelong habit of recording the names of everyone he met.

He attended church every Sunday and was active in a number of church youth groups as well as in the Protestant ministerial association.[4] His father introduced him and Robbie to the Sunday evening People's Forum at the Church of the Messiah, a Unitarian congregation, where they heard speakers such as Bertrand Russell and S.K. Ratcliffe of the *Manchester Guardian*. Until the Depression, summer jobs were plentiful; if one lived with one's family and spent little on entertainment, it was possible to earn enough to cover tuition and expenses for the following year. Summer employment also provided a variety of experiences. Macleod devoted two summers to selling Wear-Ever aluminum cookware, the first summer in Montreal and area, the other in Milltown, New Brunswick. There a layoff of workers demonstrated vividly to him how unemployment affected workers' purchasing power.

From June to August 1925, the twenty-year-old Macleod served as a worker-teacher at the Frood Mine in Sudbury, Ontario, under the auspices of Frontier College. When he first wrote to the college in March, he was informed that the teachers, whether university graduates or undergraduates, went to the camps as manual labourers. They were given a job like any other labourer and paid the same wage, but they were expected in addition to hold classes five nights a week in the bunkhouse. For this, if their services were deemed satisfactory, they were paid anywhere from $22 to $28 per month and provided transportation. At the end of every month they were expected to turn in a detailed report of their activities to Frontier College.

Three letters survive in Macleod's files from his stay at the Frood Mine. They provide an insight into his spiritual development and his growing commitment to the Social Gospel. The first, addressed to his brother Kenneth, dated 18 June 1925, was a description of his daily routine, the mine, and the processing of the ore. Of his own work he wrote: "Yesterday and today I have been doing plumbing work. A man called Sam and I have had to put in a whole water system – pipes, washbasins, etc. in the clubhouse where about ten of the gentlemen employees of the company live. I'm glad that I had to do it, because I've learned a lot. I can make nuts and bolts and thread pipes and lots of things like that. A few days ago I was working in the blacksmith shop and it was good fun too."[5]

Three days later, he wrote to his mother:

It has been an eventful week in many ways. Last Sunday evening was one I shall never forget.

It started by a few of us sitting around listening to two chaps yarn about their war experiences and from that developed into a discussion of the whole question – whether war was of any value in the settling of international disputes, and what a man should do if he believed that war was wrong. I didn't push the talk one bit – it is really a live issue and at least once or twice a week since I have been here I have heard the fellows talking about it. Certainly now the time is ripe to push the whole question home, when there is interest in it and there still are around men who have been through it because they are the ones who

Wendell as worker and Frontier College teacher, Frood Mine, Sudbury, Ontario, 1925 – washing up and in working gear.

are strongest in their denunciation of the whole system of the military. Then on Monday evening we had a renaissance or revival of learning in Frood – the cook, his two sons, who have been attending right along, and about three or four other men who dropped into our class-room after the regular class was over and when a few of us were still sitting around, and we talked about all kinds of things from Bolshe-vism to the advantages of education. Oh these fellows are a lean lot – they snap up every little thing in the line of current history, etc.

The labour situation is depressing. Sudbury, at the moment, has a moving population of 15,000, and on Saturday nights one can almost sense an atmosphere of dejection, even by walking along the streets – crowds of men shuffling along with no particular destination. Our mine is four miles from town, but on Thursday, I am sure a hundred men called and stayed around for a while in the hope of getting a job. Some went into the office and offered to do anything for a dollar a day. I don't know what's going to happen – if they started looting the odd store, there's no knowing what might happen. When a man is hungry he is game to do anything – even if it is only to divert his attention.[6]

Macleod's third letter, his report to Frontier College on his activities, is an illuminating social document.

Anyone who has done FC work will realize the difficulty of summarizing, at all adequately, four months of activity in a mining camp. Frood Mine is four miles from the town of Sudbury, and our camp was composed of three groups of men, each living in separate buildings – about 30 men working for the Mond Nickel Co., and about 20–30 working for the International Nickel Co., and the Smith and Travis Diamond Drill Co. I began work on Friday noon (May 22) and Friday evening I secured my first pupil. However, following advice given to me in Toronto I did not start class work until a considerable number of men had enrolled. Actual instruction began on June 1. At first my intention was to group the pupils into two classes, alternating by evenings, but later I found it better to have men come as often as possible, and so I set five attendances a week as an ideal. Inspection of the attendance record reveals the fact that of the ten men who first started only six continued to attend. The others probably were only attracted by the novelty of the thing. It was not long before I realized that my time could best be spent, not in awakening enthusiasm in study, but in assisting to study those who already were keen on further educating themselves. This meant that the number of individuals receiving instruction would have to be smaller, but that they would receive a much more thorough training. Many people feel that the great weakness of our modern educational systems is that the pupil is simply told facts instead of being guided in discovering them for himself. And so I think it is of far greater benefit for a man that he should puzzle out one single problem in fractions for a whole evening and reason the problem out for himself than that the instructor should show him how to do one example and he then work out mechanically a whole exercise of similar problems. The length of time that an instructor has with the average pupil in a camp such as ours is so limited that the amount of actual knowledge he can impart is indeed small, and in my opinion, of secondary importance. What he can hope to do is to teach a few men to think independently, and to set them on the road of studying by themselves so that when they no longer have a guide they may continue alone with the textbook. And so to overcome the pedagogic error of spoon feeding I encouraged the men to work often by themselves in their own rooms instead of coming to the classroom. From the progress made, and the consistent way in which some of these men worked, I am now satisfied that the success of this method justified its adoption.

August saw the departure of many men for various reasons. Some went to the harvest, a few to Rouyn, and several left when the brick-layers finished their work in the yard. This migration depleted my classes to such an extent that on the 18th they were given up. Much time was spent in informal discussion from this point on. Groups on the veranda in the evening and in the bedrooms just before retiring were the scene of much profitable conversation. The range of subjects covered in these periods was wide, but I found an especial interest in labour problems, our economic system, war, religion, race conflict, evolution, etc. In these groups too, I sometimes gave informal instruc-tion in such things as elementary physics and physiology and astron-omy. Of one thing I am certain, the broader a man's knowledge, the more useful he can make himself in this work. From the first of July on I took my lunch to the mine in order to get to know better the men on my gang, and the lunch hour discussions were most profitable. A keen interest in politics was developing in September, and my ignorance in this sphere often made me ashamed of myself.

Three things seem to me to be most harmful to these men, robbing them of their ambition, efficiency and money – booze, whores and poker. If the FC man is in any way to represent a higher culture, and if he has at heart the interests of the men he is working with, he must take a definite stand against these things. He can do that tactfully without pussyfooting, and may be of as much value in helping men fight these things as by giving them intellectual food. The greatest obstacles in FC work at Frood I found to be (1) proximity to Sudbury, (2) the fact that there were four different shifts with a weekly rotation, (3) the constant coming and going of men to the camps.

The greatest remuneration the FC instructor receives is the friend-ship and gratitude shown to him by some of the men he has been able to help. Many a young man in our Northland grows up and goes through life without knowing what it is to have a real pal. Brought up on a farm, living with foreign born parents and then going to the bush or the mine, instead of to school, he has no chance of enjoying the social benefits of community life. Just one unit in a great struggle for existence in which the better educated or the man with specialized training wins out. He is handicapped before he is born. The most worthwhile thing the college man in camp can do is to be a comrade to such lads, using all the sympathy and intelligence at his disposal to show them that life is more than a vicious race, and that some kindness and justice still remain in the world. The University man's training at home and at school peculiarly fits him to be this kind of friend.

One or two days after I had arrived at Frood I was unloading a freight car of bricks with a young lad who had come from a background like that described. I heard him stop and say to another fellow – there are forty bricks in a row, the pile is ten deep and nine high; how many bricks are there left in my end of the car? That night going home I asked him how he would like to be able to do that kind of calculation himself. He replied: "By gee, I can't even read or write." It was a month before I could rid him of the idea that he was a dunce! Before he left he had written letters home and could read easy English.

This inferiority complex is found often among some of the Poles. When a man is constantly told that he is not a "white man," and constantly treated as an animal, deep down in his heart he begins to wonder whether perhaps after all he is a kind of lower being. One of my best chums was an Austrian of 27 who had come to this country at the age of 16. He had little schooling, but by hard plodding had worked himself up in engineering until he had received 3rd class papers. His ambition was to marry, have a comfortable home and to educate his children along truly noble lines. Being a man of higher sensitivities and of natural refinement, the rough camp environment grated on him and he tried to make friends in more cultured circles of society. But then he was so frozen out, his foreign ancestry being constantly hurled at him, and given so many unkind rebuffs that now he believes the whole world to be selfish and cruel. Social barriers prevent him from mixing with "decent" Canadian families, so that now he has abandoned all hope of home and family and has sunk into a state of indifference and pessimism that is damnable. What that man and others of his type need is friendship and a little touch of family life. I am sure that there must be some good people in Sudbury – people in the churches who are more than nominal Christians – who would welcome such men into their homes if only for Christmas or the occasional Sunday dinner. I have been wondering lately whether the FC man situated near a town as I was, could not bring these two groups together. I wish I could live the summer over again and try out something like that. I think it has great possibilities.[7]

The link with Frontier College, begun in 1925, lasted Macleod's entire life. On the organization's eightieth anniversary in 1980, its newsletter, *Frontiers*, recorded that at the annual meeting "Dr. J. Wendell Macleod, a labourer teacher in 1925, reflected upon his earlier and continuing involvement with FC, as well as his association with his friend and colleague Dr. Norman Bethune who was a fellow FC worker in 1911."[8]

In September 1926 Macleod attended a month-long seminar in Algonquin Park with students from across North America. Organized by the Student Christian Movement, the seminar was led by Henry Burton Sharman, and its goal was "to scrutinize the Synoptic Gospels to discover a convincing interpretation of the Man of Nazareth and the relevance of the message to life today."[9] Sharman was a remarkable man, an agricultural chemist who abandoned science for a scientific study of religion – in the person of Jesus – and to analyse critically the synoptic gospels. He became very active in the student volunteer movement of North America and later in the Student Christian Movement (SCM) in Canada.

Macleod became a member of the SCM when he began university, and he remained a member for many years. Founded in 1921 at the first Canadian National Student Conference at Guelph, Ontario, the SCM defined itself as "a fellowship based on Christian conviction and concern" and as "being concerned with understanding our world and society, and the Christian faith." It had its origins in the post–World War I climate, when there was a growing concern for the inequities and injustices within Canadian society and between nations.

He spent a further summer as a waiter at the Manoir Richelieu on the lower St Lawrence, but it did not pay well, as a typhoid epidemic had blighted the season.

Macleod once remarked that obstetricians and pediatricians showed more concern for preventive services and community needs than did physicians and surgeons. His own instructor in obstetrics, H.M. Little, was responsible for organizing the clinics for prenatal care in the poorer parts of the city under the aegis of the Montreal Maternity Hospital. In 1925 there were 445 home confinements without a maternal death. Macleod recounted how one morning Dr Little asked the class how many had attended a forum the previous evening on arrangements for maternal and child care in the Soviet Union. He was scornful when only two students, Jim Quintin and Wendell Macleod, reported having done so. At the end of term, both got high marks.

That fall Macleod became president of the McGill Labor Club. The new secretary was David Lewis, who in 1971 would succeed T.C. Douglas as federal leader of the New Democratic Party. Lewis was dedicated, informed, and articulate, and Macleod's admiration for him never waned. "Compared with David," he later wrote, "I felt a dilettante."[10]

In 1928, Mary McGeachy Schuller, who worked for International Student Service in Toronto, offered Macleod a summer job in the ISS office in Geneva. The first woman diplomat of Canada, she spent ten years with the League of Nations as a liaison officer for the British Dominions. In 1942 she was appointed first secretary of the British embassy in Washington. This appointment made her Britain's first woman diplomat.

The only drawback of the job she offered to Macleod was that he would have to arrange his own transportation. He and a friend, Martyn Estall, spent a week walking up and down ship gangplanks in the Montreal harbour before they finally landed jobs aboard the SS *Gundulic*, a Yugoslav tramp steamer. They were hired to replace several sailors who had jumped ship on arrival in Montreal. Macleod recalled their adventurous passage:

As we proceeded from Montreal to Quebec City, the captain must have concluded that we were good for more – and had us standing behind the sailor at the wheel. After we dropped the pilot at Father Point the captain had us take turns at the wheel. For a month we crossed paths every four hours between foc's'l and bridge. One day when we were in warmer waters off the Azores headed for the Straits of Gibraltar, the captain who was amidships suddenly shouted "Look (as in "Luke") at the sun there! it should be there!" (10–15 degrees off course). My error was to pay more attention to my Italian phrase book than to the needle of the compass. I would have been fired at once had we not been shorthanded. Several days later we reached Oran and then Palermo where we got our discharge and certificate.[11]

Macleod worked in Geneva for the summer, attended a conference in Chartres, went hiking in the Alps with his brother Robbie and a friend, visited Munich and Freiburg, and then worked his way back to Montreal, washing dishes on the SS *Canadian Traveler*, a freighter sailing from Antwerp. The high point of this summer was getting to know French and German students at the international conference at Chartres. Discovering Europe in this way, he reflected, "seemed worth many months of study in one's home university." He always remembered that summer as his *annus mirabilis*; it was his last summer vacation for some years.

He graduated from McGill in 1930, winning the Holmes Gold Medal for the highest aggregate standing in the four years of medicine and the Stewart Prize "for presenting in every respect the highest qualifications to practice his profession" – neither of which he felt he deserved. He wrote that he was "very surprised" by the Holmes Gold Medal, though, on reflection, "not surprised in some ways ... several bright students left the class for a variety of reasons."[12]

By starting his internship one month early after graduation, he was able to arrange to spend October in Western Canada. "This was by way of being an escort in one car of a trainload of Chinese labourers going through to Vancouver in bond to join their families after working many years as labourers in European post-war reconstruction," he explained in an interview years later. "It permitted stops in half a dozen western cities and Toronto on the way home. One stop, at Dr. Archer's United Church Hospital in Lamont, Alberta, permitted my delivery of a baby in a German homestead on the prairie."[13]

He visited North Battleford and went on to Hafford, Saskatchewan, by train. There he spent three days and attended a horse auction where most of the people were Ukrainians or Russians. In Winnipeg he met William Boyd, an Edinburgh pathologist and a famous teacher. Invited to Professor Boyd's house for a martini, he met Lennox Bell and Harry Botterell. Bell later became a professor of medicine and dean of the University of Manitoba Medical College, and Botterell became dean of medicine at Queen's University in Kingston. While in Winnipeg, Macleod attended a meeting at the Ukrainian Labour Temple and learned about the Winnipeg General Strike of 1919, which led him to reflect that his immersion in medicine had made him lose sight of social events and issues.

On his return to Montreal he found his father booked for hospital with an advanced malignancy. Sadly, John Macleod did not survive. In 1931, with Helena Macleod a widow and Kenneth and Archie still in their teens, Wendell Macleod decided to remain in Montreal for at least another year.

He was a junior intern at the Royal Victoria Hospital in 1930–31 and a resident the year after. It was during this time that he met Norman Bethune. Macleod had developed an interest in tuberculosis after spending a month at the Laurentian Sanatorium in 1929 and another month in 1930. He attended some cases with Bethune, who was experimenting with various ways of resting the affected lung in patients with tuberculosis, using oil instead of air for pneumothoraces. Macleod found him an exciting and exhilarating teacher. Bethune then went to Detroit to set up a surgical practice, and they did not meet again until 1934.

Considering Macleod's interest in tuberculosis, Dean C.F. Martin suggested that he spend a year or two at Harvard, Johns Hopkins, or even Philadelphia, where the Phipps Institute was advanced in its studies of the disease. Though he considered Martin "a very wise man," Macleod chose instead to follow the advice of J.C. Meakins, who suggested a residency in internal medicine under his friend David Prestwick Barr, head of medicine at the Washington University Medical Center in St Louis, Missouri. Macleod spent 1932–34 at Washington University and the Barnes Hospital in St Louis. He greatly admired Barr, whom he found accessible, egalitarian, and a man of broad interests: "He took me for what I was – earnest, friendly, one who had respect for and got on well with patients."[14] Macleod's subsequent interest in gastroenterology was a "kind of accident," recommended by Barr for his second year in St Louis.

It was in St Louis in late 1933 or early 1934 that Macleod met Margaret Wuerpel, an art major with a bachelor's degree from the University of Wisconsin and a master's degree in the history of art from Mount Holyoke College in Massachusetts. Margaret's sister was a docent at the art gallery Macleod often visited on his days off, and she introduced him to Margaret, who was working as an assistant. Their father was of German-French origin, a professor of art at St Louis, and very old-fashioned. Their mother was from Vienna. By all accounts Margaret was a lively and gifted young woman. Macleod was "completely charmed" by her.

In May 1934 he invited her to a concert. The program was Beethoven's Seventh Symphony. When they arrived, the weather was appropriately warm and spring-like, but when they emerged after the concert

Wendell and Margaret Macleod, wedding day, St Louis, 1935

they found the ground covered with snow. The event lingered in Macleod's memory as a metaphor for their subsequent relationship.

He did not see Margaret again until about a month before he was to return to Montreal. A psychiatrist at Barnes informed him that she was in the psychiatric ward suffering from severe depression and suggested that Macleod might drop in on her. He became a regular visitor. During one of his visits, when he had fallen quiet, she said, "A penny for your thoughts."

He responded, "I think it might be a good idea if we got married."[15]

She accepted, and "her condition improved promptly after that." They agreed to marry the following spring.

Chapter Two

The Montreal Years, 1934–1941

———□———

HAVING SPENT TWO YEARS in St Louis, with visits to hospitals in Chicago, Boston, and New Haven, Macleod returned to Montreal in October 1934, planning to establish a practice in internal medicine and work in gastroenterology. In 1935 he was appointed a clinical assistant in medicine at the Royal Victoria Hospital and invited to join a group of physicians working out of 1390 Sherbrooke Street West. They included Dr Brow, Dr Miller, and Dr Tidmarsh. They were not a real group but rather private practitioners who shared the same premises and divided the costs. When Tidmarsh left for a year, Macleod took his place and became the gastroenterologist. He also did his own x-ray work.

Social issues or ethics did not enter much into his colleagues' consideration, he found. He made house calls for the senior members of the group, and when he asked one of them how much he should charge for his services, the answer was, "A little more than you think you can get." The full rate was $5, but he often settled for $4 or even $3 if that was all the patient could afford.[1]

He and Margaret Wuerpel were married in April 1935. Macleod earned $1,400 his first year, and the couple received a wedding present of $1,000 from Margaret's mother, even though she did not really approve of Macleod. The couple bought an old car for $150 in St Louis and drove it to Montreal, where they also bought an aged Rolls-Royce previously owned by Sir Vincent Meredith. They paid $105 for it and for two years owned two cars.

Their social life was busy. Margaret wanted to pursue her interest in art, and some of the Montreal painters, especially Anne Savage, were kind to her. She was invited to see the Van Horne Collection by Adaline Van Horne and subsequently gave a number of talks there.[2] The couple also attended meetings of the League for Social Reconstruction together – sometimes arriving in the Rolls, which appealed to Macleod's sense of irony.

The LSR was inspired by University of Toronto historian Frank Underhill and by F.R. Scott, a poet and later a distinguished legal scholar at McGill. It spread rapidly, forming branches throughout the country and soon becoming the seedbed of Canadian democratic socialism, enunciating much of the program of the Canadian Commonwealth Federation (CCF) as well as social welfare and fiscal ideas. It argued along socialist lines that production for use should replace production for profit, and that monopolies must be nationalized and the economy directed by central planning, with a welfare system, worker participation in management, and civil rights guarantees.[3]

Although many leaders in the movement were academics, they constituted a small minority of the LSR's membership. Perhaps even more important were proponents of the radical Social Gospel such as King Gordon, a clergyman; Eugene Forsey, a layman in the United Church and later a McGill professor and a penetrating scholar of government; Escott Reid and Graham Spry, both future diplomats; and J.S. Woodsworth, founder of the CCF. Although Macleod never became an official member of the league, he was influenced by its ideas, particularly the residual Social Gospel values he could relate to from his own Christian reformist background.

Norman Bethune had by now reappeared in Macleod's life. "Beth," as he was affectionately called, had returned from Detroit, where he had set up a surgical practice. Soon after arriving in Detroit, he discovered that he had tuberculosis himself, gave up his practice, divorced his wife to "set her free," and entered a sanatorium. There he opted for surgical treatment – a radical procedure at the time – and made a quick recovery. He returned to Montreal in 1934 to learn more about the surgical treatment of pulmonary disease from Dr Archibald at the Royal

Victoria. The two men turned out to be incompatible, however, and
Bethune moved to Sacre Coeur Hospital, where he quickly established a
reputation as a brilliant and innovative surgeon.[4]

In 1934 Bethune invited Macleod to join a study group on the unemployed – "a tremendous experience," Macleod later recalled.[5] The com-
position of the group was fluid, and various people came and went.
They included public health nurses Libbie Park and Irene Kon, internist
Hy Shister, and neurologist Francis McNaughton. Libbie Park, later
co-author of the book *Bethune: The Montreal Years* with Macleod and
Stanley Ryerson, described Macleod during this period as "earnest,
jolly, full of enthusiasm, a hard-working general physician who fulfilled
his responsibilities to the group."[6]

Although the members held different political and philosophical
views, what brought them together was a common concern over the de-
plorable condition of the health of the people, the paucity of medical
services available to them, and the economic problems of the medical
and allied professions. Initially they met at Bethune's apartment on Fort
Street. Bethune was not in private practice, but the three hospital appointments he held provided enough for him to live comfortably. There
were never more than ten or twelve persons at the meetings, which,
chaired by Bethune, were characterized by intensive studies and discussion; they certainly were not social gatherings. Macleod was inspired by
Bethune's declaration, "You've got to be a hustler and do things – you've
got to cast your vote – don't wait for the crowd." Since by his own account Macleod was a procrastinator, the advice had an impact. In retrospect he saw this experience as "important in breaking through to the
real world."[7]

As Bethune's conscience became increasingly politicized, he considered joining the Communist Party but didn't think he was sufficiently self-
disciplined. He was given to making inflammatory remarks about social
issues, leading his Montreal colleagues to consider him something of a
loose cannon. According to Macleod, it was Stanley Ryerson, a Toronto
historian and a leading Canadian Marxist, who deserved the credit for
getting Bethune to settle down and turn his attention to health-care delivery. Bethune was outraged by the terrible conditions that poor people
were living under. In August 1935 he attended a Physiological Congress
in Russia and was impressed by the strides the Soviets were making in
social medicine. In December of that year he participated in a sympo-

sium sponsored by the Medical Chirurgical Society (Med-Chi) of Montreal, which also featured talks by the eminent researcher Hans Selye, the endocrinologist J.S.L. Browne, and David Slight.

Bethune's talk was a paean of praise for the Soviet system: "It is the passionate belief of communists that the degrading poverty of modern life is not the will of God but the wilfulness of man. But to those noble and courageous hearts who believe in the unlimited future of the human race, its divine destiny which lies in its own hands to make of itself what it will, Russia presents today the most exciting spectacle of the evolutionary, emergent and heroic spirit of man which has appeared on this earth since the Renaissance. To deny this is to deny your faith in man, and this is the unforgivable sin, the final apostasy."[8]

Having by this time joined the Communist Party, Bethune began to collect information on alternative systems of medical care in different countries. He decided to enlist the help of his friends in making a systematic study. His goal was to examine medical and health services in developed countries and their relationship to the state, to be used as a basis for proposals on medical and health services for Quebec.

Group members individually undertook to examine the health-care systems of specific countries and to report back. Macleod chose Denmark, Hy Shister took France, and Bethune took Britain and the Soviet Union. In April 1936, Bethune described the work of the group at a Med-Chi meeting, and they subsequently adopted the title "Montreal Group for the Security of the People's Health." In July 1936 they circulated their first set of proposals to the medical and related professions. With a Quebec provincial election pending in August, they worked hard to prepare a definitive set of proposals offering four alternatives.[9]

The first was a system of municipal medicine supported by municipal taxes and provincial grants. Full-time teams of doctors, nurses, and dentists would be created to meet the needs of the citizenry. They would be provided with a small, modern hospital in which to do their work. They would be on salary.

The second alternative was a compulsory insurance scheme that would include all wage earners. It would be tried out in a municipality with a relatively homogeneous economic pattern where relief recipients were at a minimum. The true costs of insurance would be established, and the actuarial calculations would determine the premium to be paid by the individual.

The third alternative was a voluntary hospitalization or health in-surance scheme envisioned for a selected urban municipality of 5,000–10,000 people.

The fourth was intended for the unemployed and was to be a province-wide medical scheme on a fee-for-service basis, with the cost borne by the province.

Under the group's plan, the first three proposals would be carried out simultaneously as controlled experiments. They appealed for a mass meeting called by the medical societies of all French and English mem-bers of the medical and allied professions, social service workers, pub-lic health officials, representatives of the Trades and Labor Council and the Federated Charities, to put forward the demands of the professions in regard to the election campaign. However, the group's recommenda-tions aroused little interest in the medical profession and came too late to have any effect on the election results.

During these years Bethune had become passionately interested in the events of the Spanish Civil War, which erupted in 1936. He was particularly disturbed by the boycott by the British and French of the Loyalist government in Spain, while the Axis powers were arming Gen-eral Franco and his fascist rebels. With his departure for Spain the study group's activities ceased.[10] Although after 1936 Macleod saw little of Bethune, the latter had a profound and lasting influence on the younger man's life. Bethune's exhortation to link the Social Gospel to action was a motivating force behind many of Macleod's words, deeds, and ideas in the years to come. He followed Bethune's activities in China with great interest.

Bethune died in China in 1939. When word of his death reached Montreal, Macleod chaired a memorial meeting held at Windsor Hall. Hazen Sise, the young Montreal architect who had worked with Bethune in the blood transfusion unit in Spain, also attended. Sise subsequently organized the Bethune Memorial Committee and persuaded Macleod to join.

In later years Macleod was instrumental in keeping the memory of the great Canadian alive. But although he recognized and respected Bethune's convictions and his willingness to act on them, he was not blind to the man's flaws. He felt that Ted Allan's chronicle of Bethune's activities in Spain, *The Scalpel, the Sword,*[11] romanticized his old friend, and he resented contemporary efforts to make Bethune into a saintly figure.

Chapter Three

The Halifax Years, 1941–1945

———□———

BY 1940 IT WAS APPARENT that Europe was falling apart. In May, Hitler's invasion of the low countries persuaded Macleod "to change from the posture of a naïve pacifist." He joined the 5th Field Ambulance and spent two weeks at Mount Bruno carrying out World War I training exercises. He soon realized their futility in the face of modern warfare.

In February 1941 at the Royal Victoria Hospital he encountered an old friend, Donald R. Webster, surgeon commander and principal medical officer (PMO) of the Naval Shore Establishment at Halifax. From Webster he learned of the need for medical officers to cope with the rising tide of illness among the young recruits and the influx of survivors from the submarine campaign. He decided to join the navy.

By now he and Margaret had two children, Wendy and Peter. The family was about to move to a semi-detached home on Côte St Antoine Road in Montreal at the end of April, but in the third week of March, Macleod went to Halifax. Margaret would pack up and follow with the children at the beginning of May, "without our competent Quebec maid." A note appended to Macleod's diary in shaky handwriting gives details: "Don Webster accompanied Margaret and the children. Don lived with us for more than a year, preparing his own breakfast and helping prepare evening meals. His generosity led, however, to bringing for dinner an exhausted officer (often nearing breakdown from overseas duty). Margaret usually rose to the occasion especially when we had a good maid (several were not – e.g., boiling woollen sweaters)."[1]

In fact Margaret did not adjust well to the move. She did not like living in Halifax. She felt lonely and isolated and found the children difficult to look after. Macleod was absorbed in navy life and enjoyed the camaraderie of his fellow officers, many of whom he had known in Montreal. She did not feel part of his social life. "It was difficult to maintain a critical interest in anything other than the war," he later recalled. "We over-anticipated the degree of social change. Finances were difficult."[2] They also had many visitors, both family and friends, adding exhaustion to Margaret's already debilitating clinical depression. On 23 May 1942, two years after the move, she committed suicide.

Macleod recorded the events of that day starkly:

– late for lunch – Margaret weary – children up early from nap – turmoil and strife.
– too rainy to go out – I retreat for a nap.
– argument re: children's supper.
– Margaret's despair over control of children – and my cold criticism of her attitude which she could only regard as indifference or apathy, or even worse.
– with a cool air she called off her going to Bunty and Geo's (Maughans') for supper – "to treat cold."
– later in her tragic despair saying she would not go to Kentville tomorrow with Elliotts and Whitelaws and me to see the blossoms.
– her warm embrace and tears and insistence that she loved me dearly. My hasty departure with Don [Webster].
– At Maughan's her laughter missed.
– If only I had phoned or left earlier.
– to 1539 at 11:15 and the crack of light under the kitchen door and the smell of gas.
– two hours with Norm ... attempting resuscitation but to no avail.
– the phone call to the folks in Boston was the hardest thing I had to do, harder than the resuscitation effort last night. Mother Wuerpel ... "I knew it would happen sometime." Lois [Margaret's sister] shrieks and collapses. Edward's [Lois's husband] reassuring call in the evening helped greatly.[3]

"The saddest thing is the failure to influence personality," Macleod wrote two days later. "M had so many loveable and talented qualities but they were sabotaged by a deeply ingrained pessimism or defeatist attitude (which her mother and sister unfortunately share). But why could I not bring to bear the insights and charity of my Christian experience in the Student Christian Movement and home? – and have changed things – by adding hope and faith? and there could hardly have been a better intellect to work on."[4]

In an entry dated Saturday, 30 May 1942, 9:40 P.M., he wrote:

Just a week ago this minute Margaret was making the second last entry in her memorable document. If I had phoned home or dropped away from the Maughans' I might have saved her – and yet as the days have gone on I'm sure that it's better for her to be at peace. She was unhappy almost constantly for two months especially about her inability to be calm and even – also because of my having drawn myself into a shell – a protective one too, but it made her loneliness and desolation almost complete. A consolation has been the recollection that 8 years ago next month she was in a similar state and made an attempt to escape at that time. Again in June 1939, after the shingles and many times since then it has been threatened.[5]

Five days later Macleod received a letter from Margaret's mother: "Mrs Wuerpel's letter of June 4 came today with such a venomous sting that I would have been crushed had I not had much inoculation. I think I can handle such things with a minimum of resentment now, but I doubt that I should take the risk of exposing the children to such instability. I would like them very much to know their grandfather Wuerpel and he has mastered self control – the letter upset mother pretty badly."[6]

Macleod's mother had come to help look after the children. Margaret's mother, who had never approved of Macleod, accused him of "willful neglect."

Macleod went on leave, accompanied by Don Webster. "Off to Pictou with Don Webster five days leave," he wrote, " amidst glorious sunshine and fresh green foliage – with a heart that was unnaturally joyous – no doubt because of a desire to flee from the bitterness and recriminations revealed in Margaret's people by the letter last night from her mother. Moreover mother's intention to stick by us, coupled with a feeling that she is equal to it, and my observation during the past few weeks that she exerts a good influence on the children – all this makes for a comforting feeling of security. Don is full of stories which are interesting and diverting."[7]

The Pictou program of rest, sleep, good food and drink, diverting company, and Don's readings from Damon Runyon helped to restore Macleod's spirits. Then, soon after his return to duty, he learned that his brother Archie was missing in action in the Near East. "What futility that Archie with his sweet and generous unselfish spirit should perish while others who have lived lives of bitterness and engendered the poison in others should live on – it is tragic," he wrote.[8] It was not until 21 August that word arrived that Archie had been shot down over North Africa but had survived and been taken prisoner by the Germans.

By September, Macleod was back in a busy clinical and social environment that helped to restore his confidence and resiliency. His agreeable personality as well as his interest and competence, and his friendship with old McGill and Royal Vic colleagues, soon led to promotion. In September he was assigned a desk job and told by Dr " Newly" Philpott whom he had known at McGill (and who later became the head of Obstetrics at the Royal Victoria Hospital in Montreal) that it was a better future for him than clinical work in the navy. But Macleod felt that a desk job brought his courage into question when he was sending others off on dangerous assignments. He thought he should be sent into action himself: "It is probably the job I should do. If I came through it I would be of more use to the navy, and my self respect would be greater. If I didn't, then my children would have no cause to be ashamed. It is hard though to distinguish self indulgence from unselfish patriotism – the latter is a rare bird."[9]

He soon got his chance. "Out of a grey sky, the SMO said, looks like a bad weekend, how would you like to go to sea tomorrow?"[10] Macleod joined the destroyer HMCS *Columbia* for convoy escort duty. Columbia had been attacked by a U-522 just two weeks previously, but the torpedo missed and Macleod's three months aboard were comparatively uneventful. When the ship stopped in New York to pick up the convoy, he visited The Cloisters at Fort Tryon Park where two years before he had been with Margaret. He "could not retard the tears in the Gothic chapel where Margaret and I had so happy an afternoon in June '40."[11]

For the next three months the *Columbia* escorted ships from New York and Halifax to Cape Race, Newfoundland, where they were taken over by another escort force. Despite initial bouts of seasickness,

Macleod enjoyed working with the crew and learning about sailing and navigation. He also had time to read, a pleasure denied him in his busy life ashore.

Shortly after his posting on the *Columbia* he was promoted to the position of command medical officer (CMO, Canadian North West Atlantic) and senior medical officer under Commodore (Halifax). Finally given an office of his own, he commented: "I hope to reach new heights of efficiency."[12]

Within a few days he received a call from Ottawa asking if he would like to attend a four-month course in tropical medicine. Although he had serious misgivings about how his absence might affect his family, he decided to go. The course in "practical epidemiology for the tropics"[13] was offered at the Naval Medical Hospital in Bethesda, Maryland. It was comprehensive and rigorous. "I feel that the bottom has been knocked out of things," he commented on 21 May. "The experience is more than just technical training – it is the basis for my intellectual renaissance and it is most essential psychotherapy."[14] He studied tropical medicine and epidemiology, statistics, and even some navigation.

As usual he soon made many new acquaintances. He visited Chestnut Lodge, one of America's foremost psychoanalytic hospitals, where he attended a seminar with Harry Stack Sullivan and came away with a copy of Dexter Bullard's lecture on "Conceptions of Modern Psychiatry." He began enjoying social events, the theatre, music, and the new National Gallery. He also felt himself attracted to some of the young women he met and realized how he longed for female companionship

On 12 August 1943 he graduated from the course, and after a leave of absence returned to Halifax where he was soon busy again with administrative and clinical duties. He received an appointment to the Penicillin Board, headed by Dr Ray Farquharson of Toronto, which was established to regulate the distribution of the new wonder drug. Macleod represented the army, air force, and navy units in Halifax and was involved in monthly meetings in Toronto.

While in Toronto in early September he had supper at the Guild of All Arts. There he met Jessie McGeachy, the younger sister of his old patron, Mary McGeachy Schuller. "Jessie is an intensely interesting and very gifted girl," he noted. It was something of an understatement. Jessie had graduated from Toronto General Hospital Nursing School in 1927 with ambitions to become a psychiatric nurse. She enrolled in a course at Cobourg, which she found unsatisfactory and did not complete. She became an office nurse to John Oile, a prominent Toronto cardiologist, who encouraged her to take pre-med studies while continuing to work for him. She did her final year at the Toronto Psychopathic Hospital, then joined the staff of the Women's College Hospital.

The day after their meeting Macleod took her to dinner at the Old Mill, "where antiquity, the claret and a climax in congeniality and appeal made it one of the finest evenings. Would that it could be continued."[15] The relationship matured at a rapid pace, and they were married on 12 February 1944 in Toronto. They returned together to Halifax, where Jessie worked in psychiatry for the remainder of the war.

On 14 October Macleod took over from Don Webster as PMO, Royal Canadian Naval Hospital, Halifax. Among his duties was writing year-end reports on the officers under his command. He noted that one man showed little sympathy for young medical officers in trouble, was severe with young officers generally, and kept them at arm's length. Macleod's report greatly offended the officer, a University of Toronto graduate who described Macleod's remarks as "unjust, dishonest and self promoting." There was considerable competition at the time, even hostility, between the graduates of McGill and Toronto; Macleod's report did nothing to ease the situation. (Two years later, when Macleod was awarded the OBE for his wartime services, he would receive a letter from a Toronto lawyer. "We all know how you got your OBE," the letter said, alluding to Macleod's friendship with Don Webster, his predecessor as PMO and a McGill graduate, who had recommended him for the award. Macleod consulted a lawyer himself, but decided to take no action.[16])

The war was finally drawing to a close. Macleod noted on 27 March 1945: "German defenses crumbling east of the Rhine and breakthrough to Berlin imminent."[17] On 7 May came "unconditional surrender – at 10:45 AM whistles blew – the fog rolled back in an unforgettable manner – the rain stopped and the sunshine began."[18] He knew he would have to spend the next few months dealing with the demobilization of his medical staff, but he began to think about his future in medicine.

In June he wrote to C.J. Tidmarsh, his former Montreal colleague, expressing his concerns about returning to the Royal Vic: "A letter from JCM [Meakins] contained the same generalities I received from him in St. Louis 11 years ago. I don't want power or a huge practice but only a chance to achieve some self expression in an intellectually active clinical department. The proper atmosphere can be achieved ... only by focussing attention on the training and development of the several med-

"He's in the Navy": Wendell with mother, Helena,
Halifax, 1944

ical generations already junior to ours. This means decentralizing responsibility, co-operative efforts at investigation and a good deal more
of departmental planning than we have seen. I think we have the crowd
to do it at the Vic provided there were an enlightened leadership! The
latter situation, quite frankly, discourages me a lot."[19]

Around this time he and Jessie received an offer from P.H. Thorlakson to join the Winnipeg Clinic. Macleod travelled to Montreal to meet
with an administrator of the clinic, Dr T. Lebbeter, to discuss the offer.
On July 28 he and Jessie agreed to accept the Winnipeg offer. On 14 August, the day of the Japanese surrender following the dropping of nuclear bombs on Hiroshima and Nagasaki, he wrote to Dr Lebbeter:

Dr Jessie McGeachy with Peter and Wendy,
Halifax, 1945

As far as we can predict our future at this time, we have decided to
accept your invitation to join the staff of the Winnipeg Clinic. The decision to forsake my old niche in Montreal, and to forego other opportunities that have opened up elsewhere, is based on the following aims:
– to practise medicine with a congenial team, being able to utilize
  modern diagnostic aids which are usually available only in group
  practice.
– to have contact with students and the life of the junior group in
  a teaching hospital.
– to plan special study and investigation in a way that is seldom
  possible in individual private practice.
– to practice medicine without encountering at every point the
  fee problem.

–   to be associated with a group who recognize the changing socio-economic structure, and who endeavour to meet it in a realistic manner.

The date of my release from the service is still uncertain. I shall be engaged in demobilizing at high speed for most of the fall, and as PMO of the hospital here, it may be hard to escape until the peak has been passed. My guess would be availability at the beginning of the year, but with the rapid change in tempo in the Pacific, it may be earlier.[20]

On 2 October his successor as head of the RCN Hospital was announced. "I am declared surplus for October 20," he said.

On 25 January 1946, Macleod was awarded the OBE. The citation read: "For outstanding service as Chief Medical Consultant and Principal Medical Officer of the Royal Canadian Naval Hospitals in Halifax. Throughout his naval career, Surgeon Commander Macleod has contributed a leadership of the highest order in the development of the Medical Services. His untiring efforts for the welfare of the Service and his personal high standard of professional skill and integrity have been an inspiration to all."

Chapter Four

The Winnipeg Years, 1945–1952

—□—

MACLEOD AND HIS FAMILY arrived in Winnipeg on 22 November 1945. "The temperature was 10 degrees," he wrote. "Had supper with Dr. Lebbeter and Dr. Thor[lakson] at the Manitoba Club. We reviewed the clinic building and were flabbergasted by its modernity, its equipment and its obvious business-like organization."[1]

The Macleods took up their positions at the clinic, Jessie with the neuropsychiatrist Gilbert Adamson. The remainder of the year and much of 1946 were occupied with finding housing, establishing a presence at the clinic, getting started in practice, and beginning to take some leadership in organizing a "scientific committee" for the clinic. They settled in, making friends, leading an active social life, happy in their marriage and getting a good deal of pleasure from the children.

Meanwhile a Saskatchewan connection made prior to leaving Halifax was continuing to grow. Macleod had received a visit from Sandy Nicholson, then a member of the Saskatchewan cabinet. Nicholson raised the possibility of Macleod joining the University of Saskatchewan's medical faculty. Macleod felt that he was not ready to take on the job. He told Nicholson that he was a better follower than a leader.[2]

On 15 November, less than two weeks before their departure for Winnipeg, he had received a letter from Dr Fred Mott in Regina. Mott, a graduate of McGill and an expert in public health matters, was advising the new CCF government of Saskatchewan on the creation of its

The four brothers – Archie, Ken, Robbie, and Wendell, 1946

health services plan. He invited Macleod to Regina to discuss the plan and College of Medicine issues with himself and Premier Douglas. Mott advised Macleod that the College of Medicine Advisory Committee was planning to meet with high-level consultants 19 and 20 November, and they wanted him to be there. The consultants were John Grant of the Rockefeller Foundation, John Leonard of the Bingham Associates Fund and Tufts Medical School, and Sam Hamilton, a leading consultant on mental hospitals (a psychiatric hospital was to be built in association with the University Hospital).

The purpose of the meeting was to broaden the vision of those who would formulate the policies for the medical school and hospital. Mott was concerned that all the planning to this point had been done by one man, Dean J.S. Lindsay. "He wants to develop a good school," Mott wrote to Macleod, "but he lacks the imagination to do the kind of planning required to measure up to the situation here. The possibilities over the years ahead here in Saskatchewan are boundless if we can develop a university centre keyed to progressive as well as scientific thinking. It is almost impossible to make any significant contribution when one is working day and night on urgent operating programs."³

Nicholson and Mott, both probably acting with the knowledge of Premier Douglas, were clearly interested in nurturing a link with Macleod and hoped to involve him with the new College of Medicine and University Hospital. In April 1947 Nicholson brought Macleod up to date on events in Saskatoon. In November he received another letter from Mott, now the chair of the Saskatchewan Health Services Commission:

There has been a bit of a lull in our medical education efforts here except that excavation work has started on the University Hospital and a very exciting visit in September by Dr. Alan Gregg of the Rockefeller Foundation accompanied by Dr. McIntosh the Canadian representative of the International Health Division ... Although I thought that Dr. Gregg would be very critical of our developing a school in Saskatchewan, he seemed to take it for granted that the school was going to go ahead, and by the time he left, he had the same gleam in his eye, if I am not mistaken, that has characterized John Grant and others who have looked into our efforts here. He came very close to making certain commitments that may be very significant in the development of the school ... he virtually agreed to take on five or six professors who might be given appointments in advance and to give them two-year fellowships for special training which would be useful in their future work. It was his recommendation that such men spend at least a full year in some major centre, rather than skipping around the world to various points.⁴

By this time Macleod was becoming disenchanted with the Winnipeg Clinic. He was particularly unhappy about its commercialism. The pressure to see patients was intense, and the predominance of the surgeons, especially under Thorlakson's autocratic rule, was apparent. There was not enough time to teach students and do research. He had been strongly tempted by Mott's announcement of the Rockefeller Foundation offer and Dean Lindsay's display of the plans for University Hospital. "Does one's destiny lie with the new medical school (and the new order) in Saskatoon?" he wondered.⁵ His enthusiasm was dampened by a revelation that the Saskatchewan government was short of cash and might not be able to complete the hospital. He was disappointed ("but relieved?").

On 30 January 1949 he wrote notes to himself on his dissatisfactions with his clinic work:

It is not constructive:
(1) too much time on rural patients who "shop" at the clinic just as they do at the Bay – who go back to no doctor and who are not able to receive enough guidance to permit a good long-term result.
(2) not enough time with the interns and students who will be the doctors of these people eventually.
(3) the clinic's policy will perpetuate or at least is not meeting in progressive manner certain vital socio-economic issues:
    – we are perpetuating the big surgical fee and thus the big political power of the surgeons
    – we look on medical care as a commodity (like beef or grain)
(4) we are not really interested in research or education. In all our major meetings there is never once a reference to research, education, duty to the med. school, or the patient's problem of cost ... We justify a particular fee by saying it is as cheap as such and such a scale of fees, referring to artificial schedules. We have never scratched our heads to see how we can lower the cost to the patient. We are in big business. We are blighted by ideological deficiency disease and that is why I feel that the clinic interferes with my feeling that I can be a *citizen* in medicine.
    The sad thing is that our clinic has come so close to being a great thing.
    – good people, good equipment and enough patients. The missing link is in the realm of motivation, and I believe that this stems from deficiencies in the leadership. Thorlakson does not seem to realize that he has doctors who care for more than:
    – good facilities for looking after patients
    – good arrangements re: salary, vacations, trips and pensions and opportunities to teach at the medical school.[6]

The breaking point came in December 1948 when he was humiliated by the clinic trustees' criticism of his operations deficit: "I feel like a 'kept woman' and am being reminded of it."[7] He celebrated his decision to leave by "listening to Gustav Mahler's symphony #2 in C major – magnificent and fitting to mark the week of our plans for emancipation from big business."[8] He realized it would be difficult to set up in practice on his own and that he would miss the advantages of the clinic, especially its ancillary services, but he was still determined to go. "The big clinics keep teachers busy doing an unsatisfactory job of treating patients who can't get good care in the country,"[9] he complained, and he felt that the discrepancy between medical and surgical fees was a large part of the problem.

"We are ending a funny year," he mused. "Cold war with Russia. The world cynical. Chiang Kai Shek folding up and Norman Bethune's team winning. Our family has its first beach vacation and Jessie and I try out oil painting. Wendy to Rupertsland school and Peter becomes a footballer and a boy. My paper to the Royal College is accepted. The big issue: how and when do we leave the clinic? Unofficial overtures – Saskatoon and Halifax."[10]

Jessie resigned from the clinic in February 1949. Dr Thorlakson characteristically attributed it to her "domestic needs," though she began making plans to open an office of her own. Macleod stayed on, essentially marking time as he waited for the Saskatchewan situation to clarify. It was an unhappy period for him as he became more and more resentful of the long working days, the endless letter-writing about patients, the impossibility of doing any scholarly work, and his own inability to make a firm decision about his future. "A helluvaday at the clinic," he wrote on 19 May 1949. "Mr. Kleiman is the klimax – I see no future in this kind of practice and this month we are financially embarrassed."[11]

In June 1949, in Saskatoon for a Canadian Medical Association meeting, he had breakfast with Fred Mott. Mott told him that the Saskatoon medical school building had been completed and work was proceeding on the hospital.

As that year passed too, Macleod summed it up: "An atomic war in our time is accepted. Canada emerges as a big little power but with juvenile control of its manpower assets. We try to sell our home but seem stuck. Jessie's practice about to start. My own pay is raised and I seem less and less equal to a move toward independence outside the clinic ... Grey hairs and the male menopause and constant fatigue and not a little psychoneurosis."[12]

The Winnipeg Flood dominated 1950. On 14 May Macleod recorded that two hundred patients from the Winnipeg General Hospital and all from Misericordia had been evacuated.[13] He spent most of the month working on flood control through HMCS *Chippewa*, the naval depot. On 17 May he noted he had spent his "first night home in eleven."[14] As

University of Manitoba Students Medical Association Annual Dinner, May 1950. Wendell, honorary president of the association, receives the gold-headed cane from his predecessor. Dr Lennox "Buzz" Bell in the foreground.

the year went on he felt increasingly tired and depressed. After a clinic meeting on finances, he wondered, "Is this a turning point or is this too late? I feel I am past my best – no spark and no groove to spark in."[15]

Then, on 17 November, he was visited by Rolf Struthers, the Rockefeller Foundation representative in Europe, who brought word of the University of Saskatchewan's medical school. He informed Macleod that Lindsay's successor must be appointed soon and that Fred Mott was not approved for the position by the medical profession. Macleod would have the "refusing of it." Macleod found this disclosure very unsettling.[16]

In his diary on 10 January 1951 he observed that it had been twenty years since his father died, then added: "Letter from Dean Lindsay in Saskatoon – am I interested in being his successor? They are calling for applicants."[17] He was indeed interested – he now felt ready for the task. He had weathered the emotional storm of Margaret's suicide. He had remarried. He had spent seven years as an internist and gastroenterologist. He had a good deal more confidence in himself. He also had a hearty dislike for the private-practice model of health care as carried out at the Winnipeg Clinic.

One feature of the offer that undoubtedly influenced him to apply was the fact that the Rockefeller Foundation was prepared to make a generous grant in support of the new school. They offered $10,000 for a year's salary and the opportunity to spend the time with Alan Gregg, director of the Division of Medical Sciences at the Rockefeller Foundation. There Macleod would have an opportunity to study the new models of medical education being developed in the United States. He would also travel to study other medical institutions. "Can our family face it?" he wondered.[18]

His social conscience as well as his experience led him to believe that he could and should make a contribution to the teaching and formation of young doctors. Later that month, in Saskatoon's Bessborough Hotel in a room with a view of the frozen Saskatchewan River, he discussed the deanship with a parade of "visitors":

My first guest was Arthur Moxon [chair of the Board of Governors of the University of Saskatchewan], a former Dean of Law and disciple of President Walter Murray. He was gracious and perceptive, and not at all like the St. James Street boys who dominated the Board at McGill and the Royal Victoria Hospital in Montreal. My next visitor was Walter Francis, a lawyer, with whom I became very friendly later on and who invited me and Jessie to join the "couples club" some years later. I found President W.P. Thompson very friendly and impressive and open-minded. He pointed out that politics would not enter into the issue of any appointment. Moxon was a Conservative, Francis was a Liberal, and he was labelled as being very friendly to the government – a CCF man. He was determined that the new College of Medicine, like the College of Agriculture, would be a service to the people of Saskatchewan.[19]

At the time of Macleod's visit the new hospital was little more than a hole in the ground. "It's minus 37 degrees outside," he noted. "We speculate on new lives." He was also concerned about Mott, who had earlier been considered for the deanship. "Where can FM go? Public Health or associate dean?"[20]

On 2 February 1951 Macleod formally applied to the University of Saskatchewan for the post of dean of the School of Medical Sciences; if that was not available, he wished to be considered for the Chair of Medicine. Dr Lindsay had indicated that there was another applicant being interviewed for the deanship.[21] He had in fact solicited at least

three other persons as possible candidates: R.B. Kerr of the University
of British Columbia, C.C. Grey of the University of Toronto, and C.B.
Stewart, a professor of epidemiology at Dalhousie University.

Lindsay also sought information on Macleod from C.J. Mackenzie,
head of the National Research Council and former dean of engineering
at the University of Saskatchewan.[22] Mackenzie responded: "Unfortunately I do not know Macleod personally, but I have heard that he is
first rate – he is being considered for the top medical position in the
Canadian Navy. Dr O.M. Solandt has a very high opinion of his personality and qualifications."[23] Lindsay replied: "WPT [President Thompson]
had a very favorable account of Macleod from Penfield."[24]

Wilder Penfield, the pioneering neurosurgeon from the Royal Vic in
Montreal, had actually expressed some doubts about Macleod's suitability. "He is perhaps too kindly disposed and too unwilling to believe
in the shortcomings of others," he wrote. "This resulted in his urging
the candidacy of certain young physicians who were accepted in the
Royal Victoria Hospital, and who, perhaps, were unwisely chosen.
This suggestion is made by someone else and not by any information of
my own."[25]

Stewart, who was turned down for the deanship, wrote that he
strongly endorsed the choice of Macleod for the job.[26]

On 27 April Macleod received a wire from Lindsay: "Appointment
approved – for July 1, 1952."

Macleod would be missed in Winnipeg. Alex Richman, a third-year
medical student at Manitoba in 1951, was a member of a clinic group
taught by Macleod, and remembered an episode in which Macleod
showed the group how to coordinate clinical events with life cycle events
in a patient using a novel approach introduced by Adolph Meyer. "The
group was impressed by Wendell's ability to display the relation between illness and 'life.' One member of the group used the term 'nervous breakdown,' and Wendell elicited the understanding of the term.
This occurred before our lectures in psychiatry. No on else displayed
bio-psycho-social relations as vividly or in such a sensitive manner."[27]

Allan Klass was a friend and colleague of Macleod's during the Winnipeg years, not a part of the Winnipeg "establishment," at least in part
because of his views, and in equal part because he was Jewish. Jews were
excluded from the staffs of the two large clinics at that time, and Klass
and a few other Jewish physicians started their own group practice clinic
(the Mall Clinic). Macleod was "highly regarded as a person," Klass said;
"his politics perhaps suspect, but he was well thought of."[28]

Chapter Five

The Saskatoon Years, 1952–1962

———□———

THE UNIVERSITY OF SASKATCHEWAN was founded in 1907, and a College of Medicine was an integral part of the early plans of its first president, Walter C. Murray. Murray believed that the university should be not an ivory tower but a practical resource to improve the well-being of the people of Saskatchewan. A medical school that would provide trained doctors and medical services for Saskatchewan would be a prime resource.

By 1926 Saskatchewan had weathered the postwar depression, its population had grown, the university had expanded, and its student population doubled. It was in this buoyant economic atmosphere that a two-year pre-clinical medical school was established. The new school followed the model advocated by Abraham Flexner, the American educator who introduced modern medical and science education to colleges and universities. It had definite prerequisites for admission; it had well-trained professional teachers in the basic sciences; and it was an integral part of the university, with which it shared its scholarly and scientific objectives. Under the guidance of Dean Stewart Lindsay, the school had quickly acquired a reputation for excellence. Only six of the 605 students who completed the two-year course between 1926 and 1954 failed to graduate.

Finding places for Saskatchewan graduates to complete the final two years of their medical course was never a problem. Most went to Manitoba, Toronto, McGill, or Alberta. In 1938, however, the University of Manitoba indicated that it would no longer be able to take its regular quota of Saskatchewan medical graduates. In the aftermath of World War II, other medical schools began making curricular changes that made it increasingly difficult for Saskatchewan graduates to meet the requirements. Dean Lindsay realized that the days of the two-year school were numbered and began to agitate for the expansion of the school to a full degree program. In this he received help from an unexpected source.

In 1942 the federal government announced that it planned to set up a national health insurance scheme. It was obvious that this scheme would call for a considerable increase in medical personnel, and a committee of the deans of medical schools and the Canadian Medical Association (CMA) advised that two new schools be set up in the provinces of Saskatchewan and British Columbia. In 1944 the Saskatchewan government granted the university the authority to establish a complete medical school and allocated $25,000 to plan a medical building on campus.

Then, on 16 June, Premier W.J. Patterson's Liberal administration was defeated by the CCF under Douglas, and the new regime decided to put things on hold while it looked at the overall health-care needs of the province. Henry Sigerist, professor of the history of medicine at Johns Hopkins University, was asked to conduct the survey. He was assisted by a group of four.[1] The Sigerist Commission reported in October 1944 and recommended, among other things, that the medical school be expanded into "a complete Grade A medical school" and that a university hospital of five hundred beds be built for scientific teaching, clinical instruction, and research.

The Saskatchewan government accepted the recommendations and in the spring of 1945 voted $100,000 to begin construction of the Medical College Building. It was expected that hospital construction would get underway at the same time. But the project faltered as the new government began to realize the enormous costs it was committing itself to. It was only through the persistent efforts of Dr Lindsay that the government was finally persuaded to go ahead. The medical building was opened in May 1950, and the University Hospital was completed in 1954, officially opening in the spring of 1955.

During the years that Macleod had been gently refusing overtures from the new socialist government in Saskatchewan, deep concerns had risen that the planning for the new College of Medicine was inadequate.

In 1950, in a confidential letter to President W.P. Thompson, Fred Mott, then deputy minister of public health, had written about the crucial importance of establishing a "first-rate school":

The task of planning for a full course of medicine is an enormous one. Here it is further complicated by the necessity for planning the associated University Hospital at the same time. Medical education is in a very fluid state today ... and we should be taking the fullest possible advantage of all the thinking and planning that has been going on in Canada, the US and abroad. This is also important from a financial viewpoint. If we can set a firm course along lines that appeal to the Rockefeller Foundation, a course that is geared to the needs of this prairie province, there might be significant financial assistance over a period of years. I think the course can be developed only by a first-rate planning team, which will have travel money available and full opportunity for consultation with leaders in the field of medical education. An approach to this task began almost four years ago when there was a slowdown in construction ... with a plan to find the right person to succeed Dr. Lindsay and to give him an opportunity to spend a year with Dr. Alan Gregg at the Rockefeller Foundation. The planning team would also contain the Professor of Social and Preventive Medicine or perhaps the Professor of Medicine and the medical superintendent of the UH. The most urgent need is to find Lindsay's successor and to get him on the job as soon as possible. If that isn't possible, we should at this stage bring in one or more highly qualified consultants to review the entire situation with us. The innate difficulties in establishing a first-rate school here are such that any serious mistake on our part might go far in creating a situation in which we might have an inferior school. Anything of the sort would be a tragic development.[2]

Mott's letter may have prompted Dean Lindsay's second approach to Macleod. On 27 April 1951 Macleod received Lindsay's confirmation that the dean's position was his. From September until July 1952 the Rockefeller Foundation would pay his salary and hoped he would use the time to travel widely and become acquainted with different patterns of medical education in the United States and Europe. Unfortunately Dr Gregg was no longer available, but the foundation would assist Macleod in planning a schedule of visits to medical schools.

The Commonwealth Fund of New York came to the rescue with a travel grant.

From January to March 1952, while still living in Winnipeg, Macleod visited medical schools in Canada, the United States, Britain, and Europe. He met a multitude of people, many of whose names he recorded in his diary, as in this excerpt from early 1952:

Glasgow – Prof. Wyburn of Anatomy is willing to reduce hours – he is broader than most.
Aberdeen – I like the departmental atmosphere of service to the people.
Edinburgh – dilemma is increased as I find a mixture of charm, professional competency but social myopia.
Newcastle, Carlisle, Manchester – an extensive list of people met, candidates identified.
London – impressed by the Hammersmith Hospital staff (John Mc-Michael, Ian Aird, Selwyn Taylor, Sheila Sherlock) – I like this place. [3]

In addition to learning about various educational plans, Macleod was assessing the people he met as possible staff for the new college. His travels were interspersed with visits back to Saskatoon to report to Lindsay and the Advisory Council of the Medical College. He also spoke to the medical communities of Saskatoon, Regina, and Moose Jaw and participated in the planning of nursing education; the Centralized Training Plan, or CTP, for nurses was under consideration at the time.

In March he left for Scandinavia, visiting Stavanger, Oslo, Stockholm, Goteborg, Copenhagen, and Aarhus, then went on to Paris, where he conferred with Rolf Struthers, a Montreal pediatrician now in charge of Europe and the U.K. for the Rockefeller Foundation. He returned to Winnipeg on 20 March, then went to Saskatoon three days later. There he conducted his first interviews with Saskatchewan premedical students, whom he found "culturally barren but sturdy."[4] In April he visited medical schools in the United States.

His interest in medical education and health as a social responsibility went back to the Montreal years when he first started in practice and was exposed to the wretched health problems of the Montreal poor during the Depression. As a member of Bethune's small group of doctors and nurses, he had studied health plans in different countries for a series of well thought-out proposals subsequently used as the basis for the first large-scale health insurance plans in Canada.

His first paper on health education and health care was given in March 1941 at a symposium at McGill (Fourth Annual Conference of Canadian Medical Students and Interns [CAMSI]) while he was still in the Naval Medical Service. Entitled "How Healthy Is Canada?," it dealt with "the inadequacy of medical care in Canada – the general problem." He identified the key issue as being that of health responsibility. "Is the health of the individual his own private problem or does it concern society as a whole?" he asked. He believed good public health service was an equal right for all and addressed some ways of accomplishing this goal. He urged the interns and medical students to turn a deaf ear to those who said it couldn't be done.

In 1947 his short article "Medicine Comes of Age" in the *University of Manitoba Medical Journal* epitomized his views on the goal of medical education: "Medicine is coming of age as a social science in the service of society. It takes a Man, not a machine to understand Mankind." He lectured and wrote about medicine's responsibility to society and the importance of inculcating these ideas into the educational process. Many of these papers were given as addresses to local medical societies in 1951–52 when he was consolidating his ideas for the curriculum of Saskatoon's new medical school. (Brief summaries of these seminal papers are found in appendix 1.)

On 24 June 1952 he submitted a substantial report to the president and board of the University of Saskatchewan detailing his plans for the medical college.[5] A distillation of his thoughts on medical education, the report is essentially the blueprint he used for creating the new College of Medicine in Saskatoon. President Thompson had it attached to the board minutes in full text. (See appendix 2.)

In it Macleod begins with the general goals of medical education and current trends, then deals with specific proposals for the University of Saskatchewan. The latter include the development of a Department of Social and Preventive Medicine, rural preceptorship, internship, the role of general practitioners in teaching, the integration of intern training and postgraduate instruction on a province-wide basis, and the appointment and organization of a full-time clinical teaching staff. The report estimates initial staff requirements and considers in detail conditions of work and remuneration of full-time staff. Financial information was based on data from other schools in Canada and the United States.

He envisaged three basic principles for the school: First, the majority of teaching would be done by full-time teachers; this was a major innovation for a Canadian medical school. Second, the concept of social medicine – the recognition of the patient as a person, the importance of the family and the community in medical care – was central to his new curriculum. His Christian upbringing and beliefs, the influence of his father, his encounter with the underprivileged and uneducated as a Frontier College teacher, his exposure to practice in Montreal, and the influence of Bethune all conspired to make this the central focus of his plans. Third, the college would be responsible for meeting the health-care needs of the Saskatchewan people.

He had visited a number of places where these concepts were being incorporated, but the institution that most influenced his thinking was Western Reserve Medical School in Cleveland. Western Reserve had put into practice some of the reforms that other medical educators had been talking about for fifty years. The objectives of the school's program were simple: "To teach medicine as a coherent meaningful whole rather than as a series of unrelated disciplines and to give the student from the beginning of his medical education a feeling for the central purpose of medicine, to deal helpfully with patients." These goals were to be attained by selecting the content of teaching for its importance and by arranging it in sequence, by rejecting any attempt to cover all fields of medical knowledge in favour of "learning to distinguish fact from theory through familiarity with the scientific method," by fostering "an understanding of the patient as a person and as a member of society," and, finally, by treating the student as "a maturing individual who could take increasing responsibility for his own education."[6]

By the start of 1953 Macleod had begun to appreciate the obstacles that stood in the way of vision. "Can we build a medical school on the shoe-string economy of the prairie 1930s?" he queried in his diary on 2 January at 1:00 A.M. "It is anachronistic and terribly frustrating and sleep dispelling. Will the hospital open in the fall of '54? If after Sept. 1, where will I get interns?"[7]

He had begun recruiting widely, from the United States, England, and Canada. Charismatic, enthusiastic, and well spoken, he projected an image of a new kind of socially proactive school and portrayed Saskatoon as an attractive place to live, with many amenities and great cultural promise. Interviewing the author in Montreal, he described his daily walk to the university from his home "through a lovely pine forest." He neglected to mention that the trees in President Murray Park were only two to three feet tall.

In short order Irwin Hilliard of Toronto was appointed head of medicine, A.B. Brown was appointed head of obstetrics and gynecology, and E.M. Nanson, a New Zealander trained in England and at Johns Hopkins in Baltimore, was appointed the head of surgery. John Gerrard of Birmingham followed shortly after as head of pediatrics, Gordon Wyant of Chicago as head of anaesthesia, and W. Feindel and J. Stratford, both of Montreal, were appointed in neurosurgery. Several junior appointments included Louis Horlick in cardiology and medicine, J.E. Merriman in respirology, and D.J. Buchan in gastroenterology.

Local physicians saw the appointments as threats to their own prospective roles in the new medical college, their status in the community, and their income. Even prior to Macleod's arrival in Saskatoon there had been apprehension about the impact of the new school. At least two senior doctors who had taught clinical diagnosis in the two-year school probably considered themselves candidates for the post of dean or professors of medicine. A tacit agreement with local doctors had apparently existed that only three full-time professors would be hired: in medicine, surgery, and obstetrics and gynecology. Macleod had not felt himself bound by that agreement.

He once described his relationship with local practitioners as following a sine wave: up and down, up and down. When he first came on the scene, everyone was welcoming and friendly. He established his basic objectives and hired the appropriate people. There were periods of crisis followed by periods of relative calm.

When the issue of privileges for local practitioners came up, his response was ambiguous. Either he and the hospital board had no clear notion of what those privileges would be or they failed to make it clear that local practitioners would have only limited privileges at University Hospital and would have to confine themselves largely to St Paul's or Saskatoon City, the two general hospitals. This resulted in a protracted struggle that attracted a great deal of public attention.

Among Macleod's most vocal and effective opponents was J.F.C. Anderson, who had been the major clinical teacher in the two-year school of medicine. A respected clinician and an influential member of the advisory committee to the college, he repeatedly cautioned Macleod that there was unease among local doctors about the role of the new school.

The "Young Turks": new faculty members of the College of Medicine, at Wendell's cottage at Wakaw in the mid 1950s. Left to right: Don Baxter, Doug Buchan, Jack Dundee, Wendell, Lou Horlick, John Merriman, Don Mitchell.

In the hope of improving the relationship, Macleod wrote at length in September 1954 to D.M. Baltzan, a senior practitioner in Saskatoon with an interest in medical education:

The medical school has been expanded not only to permit students to complete their medical education in their home province but also to participate in the extension of health care facilities and the elevation of standards of medical care throughout Saskatchewan. The task depends on the establishment of good relationships between medical college teachers and practising doctors. In the end, history will judge our undertaking on the basis of the quality of the contribution made by the university medical centre to the medical life of Saskatoon and by the quality of contributions from the Saskatoon profession to the educational and scientific activities of all its institutions.

I am well aware of the apprehension that many must feel by the delay of the University Hospital (UH) in setting forth its organizational and operational plans. To some it may seem that either time is being wasted or a Trojan Horse is being built. Neither is the case. There are many complicated problems to be dealt with and some are taking longer to work out because we are determined to avoid errors that have been made in other centres.

In an enterprise of this sort, it is inevitable that ill-founded rumours give rise to unnecessary anxiety. I would like to quote from a resolution of the Advisory Council of the College of Medicine (March 11, 1953) subsequently approved by the University Board of Governors and the UH Board as guiding principles to be observed in setting up the clinical departments in the University and Hospital.

1. Cases received in the OPD should be referred by physicians or their representatives.
2. Consultation fees charged by members of the teaching staff in connection with either in-patients or out-patients should be within the range accepted as normal.
3. Patients in the UH are likely to be subject to additional consultations in connection with the training of students, house officers or junior staff. This shall not result in penalizing the patient or the insurance scheme by the accumulation of excessive charges.
4. A stable income for full-time teachers shall be ensured. In all probability this will be lower than the income of outside practitioners in a comparable field.
5. Since this is primarily a teaching hospital, all cases should be available for the normal teaching and research activities of University Hospitals.
6. The UH Board will be responsible for the standard of medical care being undertaken.

Before closing I would like to mention one point on which I have had personal anxiety. It concerns our recently appointed clinical professors. They are all clinicians and look forward to doing clinical work when the UH is opened. At the moment there appears to be uncertainty on the part of the practising doctors as to their availability for consultation, and there is uncertainty on the part of the professors as to their eligibility to see patients in the other hospitals. The role of the teacher in another hospital is that of a consultant, not an attending physician or surgeon.

This letter, I repeat, has been written on my own initiative and without the knowledge of the teachers involved. I am sure that it will be construed in the spirit which prompted me to raise the issue –

merely one of deep concern that we do our utmost to ensure success of a venture which belongs to all of us.[8]

Macleod's overture failed. A month later the general practitioners presented a brief to the Education Committee of the College of Physicians and Surgeons of Saskatchewan. They expressed concerns about the lack of information as to where they would fit into the organization with respect to staff positions and teaching: "We feel that there is a great need for more good family doctors in this country and especially in this province. We feel that the filling of this need should be the chief educational objective of this School of Medicine. To implement and fulfil this objective we consider it necessary that the UH administration should include a department of General Practice such as that recommended by the Joint Committee on Hospital Accreditation. Having such a department at UH would make possible the undergraduate teaching of students by and for general practitioners. It would give the student the general practitioner's slant on medical practice, and a better knowledge of what general practice is like."[9]

Macleod responded:

We are in an area of concern over certain trends in medical care which can be designated the mechanical, the mercenary and the fragmenting – the latter having to do with an excessive fragmentation of labour. This concern has given rise to many corrective moves in medical education, in hospital organization and in medical economics. Our school entered its planning phase when on all sides there was a clamour to define more clearly the role of the family doctor, and to study his undergraduate preparation as well as his subsequent refresher work while in practice. Along with this has been the demand that medical education strengthen the bond between doctor and patient, stressing the more personal aspects of medical practice. So, as a school, we are committed to the preparation of family doctors for work in this province. As a corollary we have an obligation to study the problems of medical care on the Canadian prairie and attempt to foresee the best possible pattern of medical care for our people in the future. Another factor that bears on the planning of our medical school is the pattern of full-time teaching in certain key positions that has come to be recognized generally as essential to success in a modern school. Although well established elsewhere, this concept is relatively new in Canada. Hence certain features of our plan may appear strange or experimental when in fact there is precedent for everything we are doing.[10]

Though the general practitioners continued to air their suspicions and complaints, Macleod did not flinch from his objective of creating a full-time core of teachers and clinicians for the new school. He succeeded because he had the support of President Thompson and the government representatives on the advisory council.[11]

His first five years as dean were busy ones. Even so, he chided himself for his slowness, procrastination, and general inefficiency as an administrator. During his entire tenure, he did not have the assistance of an administrative assistant or a vice dean. Sidney Inskip played an important role in dealing with student affairs, and Alice Cameron did the secretarial work, but all the significant work and decision-making fell to him. He sought on several occasions to hire an administrative assistant but could never persuade the university of the necessity.

His unhappiness with the situation prompted a memo to President Thompson: "I wonder if you are as worried as I am over my loss of grip on a number of important responsibilities in my field. It seems that I am not only more behind than ever but am actually less effective in making use of what time I have in getting things done. As the person most familiar with my assets and limitations and with the deadlines I am failing to meet, perhaps you would give me your frank advice."[12]

Thompson's handwritten reply was marked "Confidential":

I should have replied to your note orally at once, but decided that if I took time to think it over I might be able to say something more helpful.

I am not at all worried on the University's behalf but only on your own. Let me say at once that I am extremely pleased with your handling of the bigger things – and they are what matter. But I have feared that you will wear yourself out with unnecessary worry and work and this may affect the smaller things.

Part of the difficulty is that of course with the College and Hospital just being organized you have far more things to look after and decisions to make than you will when they settle down into working routine.

Official portrait as dean of medicine, University of Saskatchewan, 1951–1962
(University of Saskatchewan Archives A-3271)

I am not in a position to say whether you can unload more onto other people. Unload all you can. Choose the right person for each thing, make it clear that he is fully responsible, and then forget about it.

Another part of your difficulty is your perfectionism. You stew too long over each matter until every facet is entirely to your satisfaction. And unfortunately in many matters we just can't get every angle precisely as we want it. A consequence is, I think, that you leave things vague for later decision. Thus many matters drag on consuming your time and effort. I advise consulting a few of the right people on each matter, getting the essential information and views. Don't bring it before a committee or other body until your mind is made up, then get a crisp clear cut decision and forget about it. Jack McKenzie [former Dean of Engineering at the University of Saskatchewan and later president of the National Research Council] once said to me that it is often better to make a decision even if it is wrong than to delay or to make a vague or partial decision.

I think that this is also tied up with the fact that you are too decent and kindly! If an administrator can't reconcile the views and desires of his colleagues with each other and some of them with his own, he mustn't let it bother him or make him feel badly or delay until he has everybody feeling happy about the matter.

On reading this over I see I have made it sound much more important than I had intended or than it really is. I wish I could be as proud of all other parts of the University as I am of the Medical College.[13]

———

Money was another issue that dogged Macleod. Clinical staff were under the general impression that he was not interested in it, that he felt career satisfaction was far more important. Some felt he had no clear policy on incomes but tended to pay people on the basis of their demands.

From the beginning, department heads were unhappy with their income arrangements. Initially they were offered a salary that consisted of an academic component and a supplement from earnings, the two making up the base salary. A third component was later added based on earnings to a designated maximum. The final component came from the clinical earnings pool, which received 80 per cent of excess earnings (that is, funds in excess of the operating costs of the department). The remaining 20 per cent went to the teaching and research pool to foster academic endeavours among the non-earning departments.

The issue surfaced in May 1955 in a memo from Drs Hilliard and Brown to President Thompson. They alleged that they were not being paid what they had been offered at the time of their appointment and that there was no uniformity in the salaries of the heads of different departments.[14] Thompson's response was to refer to a motion passed by the Board of Governors on 1 June 1953, "that the initial university salary of the heads of the departments of medicine, surgery and obstetrics be $10,000 with a total income of $15,000. The difference between these two figures will be made up by consultation fees ... Excess earnings beyond the ceiling should be available for the work of the department and for the creation of a teaching and research fund."

He was confident, he said, "that any other interpretations of oral statements must be misunderstandings of what was said or intended." He offered to meet with the complainants to try to resolve the issue, adding, "Since a good deal is being made of comparisons of the remuneration of different persons, I am tempted to point out that neither the Dean of Medicine nor the President of the University is now receiving as much as the head of any clinical department. It is probable that we don't deserve any more than what we are getting! But it is also probable that most people would think the comparison should be in our favour."[15]

When the new appointees had joined the university, they signed a contract allocating their clinical earnings to the university. They then negotiated the arrangement referred to in Thompson's memo. But they soon discovered that they were not receiving the annual increments awarded to regular faculty, and that their academic salaries were lower than those of people of equivalent rank in the rest of the university. Further, the budgets being allocated to them were insufficient to allow them to equip their departments properly or engage in research. A delegation led by Dr Feindel met with President Thompson and Vice-President Colb McEown. McEown made the university's position clear: "The clinical earnings are not yours; they belong to the university."

The result of this policy was that for years departmental growth and research were tied to the earnings of the departments. This fostered an undue interest in creating more clinical earnings, to the detriment of academic activities.

As his diary reveals, Macleod worked long days, often until three or four in the morning. He resented anything that took time away from his professional work and reading – even working in his garden, which he loved. His involvement in the school left him little time left to spend with his family. While Jessie was establishing herself in practice in Saskatoon, the children were growing up, and Jessie, resentful of Macleod's frequent absences and chaotic work habits, felt that he did not provide her or the children with enough support. She shared neither her husband's political philosophy nor his intense admiration for T.C. Douglas. Macleod's diaries indicate that he was aware of the problem but felt helpless to do anything about it.

In spite of this, he and Jessie found time to participate in the social life of the community – a community restricted for a number of years because of the town-gown enmity engendered by the arrival in Saskatoon of so many new doctors. The new arrivals were socially ostracized and forced to create their own social circle. This forged strong bonds among the newcomers, resulting in an active and socially rewarding community life. It also had the effect of creating a powerful esprit de corps that effectively countered the hostility of the town doctors.

In the summer of 1958 Macleod and Jessie took the rare opportunity to participate in a World University Service Committee (WUSC) student seminar in Yugoslavia. Its objective was to bring Canadian students and professors into informal contact with their colleagues in other countries, thereby affording them insights into the problems and attitudes of other nations and also interpreting Canada to the people of the world. The Canadian delegation, made up of thirty-five students, was led by J. Francis Leddy, dean of arts at Saskatchewan, and also included four senior faculty from other Canadian universities. Two University of Saskatchewan students, Richard Rempel (history) and Bob Reich (medicine), participated.

The Canadian delegation spent a ten-day orientation period in England, where Macleod introduced the group to the intricacies of English social and political life. "Although he was not a graduate of a British university," Rempel later recalled, "he provided an open, insightful and interesting account of British culture."[16] The group then spent a week in Belgrade, where they were briefed by Yugoslav academics and politicians. Yugoslavia had been chosen as the conference site because it was unique in being a socialist country that had liberated itself from the Soviet empire.

The group divided into three, touring different areas in Yugoslavia and ending up in Dubrovnik, where a seminar was held with students from several other countries. There was a good deal of international unrest at the time, and concern that Russia might invade Yugoslavia. Tension was high among the students, and some wanted to abort the visit, but Macleod exerted a calming influence. Rempel recalled that Macleod "knew as no one else in authority just how to deal with the students' anxieties and emotional exhaustion. Jessie helped with student health problems, but Wendell [rather than the somewhat aloof Dean Leddy, one of the leaders of the delegation] was in charge. He was also wise in grasping our sadness at departing from new-found friends and the enormity of the intellectual and emotional experience for us young Canadians."[17]

In his 1959 Report to the President, Macleod outlined his plans for a Department of Social and Preventive Medicine, intended from the start as a keystone of the new school:

My earliest plans for the full medical course included a Department of Social and Preventive Medicine. The specifying of social medicine in its title indicated the desire to exceed the scope of many a traditional department of public health. It was expected that ours would be vitally concerned in the appropriate relating of the medical college to the health problems of the community. Considering the social orientation of the prairies, the sensitivity of the university to community needs and the general climate of civic responsibility in health matters, it is anomalous indeed that this department was not established until 1958. Two factors were responsible: (a) a scarcity of available candidates with a clear conception of the broader mission of the medical school in Saskatchewan, and of the special role in leadership which the department should play in the school, and (b) a period of preoccupation with the organization of the clinical departments and the getting going of the new hospital.[18]

Macleod had found his candidate for professor and head of the newly established Department of Social and Preventive Medicine in Alexander ("Sandy") Robertson. With a background in academic teaching (three years at the London School of Hygiene and the Royal Free Hospital

Giving the convocation address
after receiving an honorary degree
from the University of Saskatchewan,
1966. (University of Saskatchewan
Archives, A4528)

School of Medicine) and clinical practice (five years in the General
Practice Teaching Unit, Edinburgh University), Robertson was familiar
with trends in preventive medicine in America. In many ways he was a
perfect fit for the job. Intelligent, attractive, sophisticated, he shared
the same social objectives as Macleod. His political bent was to the left.
He had no use for the "fee-for-service" method of paying doctors. His
ambitious plans for the department included adding an epidemiologist
and a sociologist to his staff and involving social workers in the teaching program.

In his initial report, Robertson wrote that what struck him when he
first entered into correspondence with Macleod in 1956 was "that the
whole thinking of the dean and senior faculty since the school was expanded, has been in terms of expecting that this department would play
a major role in the development of the school. In many medical schools,
Departments of Preventive Medicine or Public Health have been fulfill-

ing secondary roles. There is little doubt that the position in Saskatchewan is different, where there is a common interest in the subject by
the majority of faculty." Robertson attributed this interest to the "special climate of this unusual province in which health services have come
to play a very important part in the community's culture," and saw social medicine as an academic discipline, built on the basic sciences of
epidemiology and sociology and having a special responsibility for the
integration of the social and clinical components of a medical student's
training. He felt there was a high degree of interdisciplinary communication at the university and that the situation was favourable for the
creation of such a curriculum. He stressed the need for at least one behavioural scientist who could provide a plan for continuous evaluation
of the curriculum.[19]

The story of the Department of Social and Preventive Medicine is
not complete without mentioning the role of Sam Wolfe, at that time a
general practitioner in Porcupine Plain, Saskatchewan. Wolfe had an
excellent reputation as a family doctor and was known for the care he
took in working up his patients before referring them to specialists in
Saskatoon.

"Sam Wolfe was our great hope," Macleod later recalled.[20] When
he, Jessie, and Robertson visited Wolfe in Porcupine Plain in an effort to
expand the preceptorship program, they were impressed. In a covering
letter to President Thompson, Macleod referred to "the kind of extension work in Saskatchewan communities which the right kind of person
could do as a preceptorship supervisor. I know that you would enjoy
meeting Sam Wolfe of Porcupine Plain some day. He is both sharp and
broad."[21]

Wolfe had an interest in psychosomatic medicine. When he expressed a wish to take further training in psychiatry, Macleod arranged
for it. Robertson was impressed with Wolfe's potential for creating a
family medicine clinic in association with the Department of Social and
Preventive Medicine and arranged for a grant from the Rockefeller
foundation that provided two years' support for Wolfe at the School of
Public Health at Columbia University.

Having achieved the initial part of his program for universal (insured)
medical care, Premier Douglas moved rapidly towards a full medicare
program for the province. He revealed the nature of it in a radio address

to the people of Saskatchewan on 16 December 1959: "If we can do this
... and I am sure we can ... Saskatchewan will lead the way. Let us
therefore have the vision and courage to make this step toward a more
just and humane society." Douglas naively believed that the government
and the doctors could reach an amicable settlement. However, the doctors were angered by Douglas's failure to keep his promise that he
would consult with them before making a public announcement of his
plan. They were adamantly opposed to any compulsory scheme that
threatened to put the medical profession under government control. A
full-fledged political battle ensued.[22]

Sandy Roberston was outspoken in his support of Douglas and his
Medicare plan and as a result was viciously attacked by the spokesper-
sons of the College of Physicians and Surgeons of Saskatchewan. J.W.T.
Spinks, who succeeded Thompson as president in 1960, did not share
the liberal ideas of Robertson and Macleod. A distinguished chemist who
had served the university in many capacities for more than a half century, Spinks was very conservative in his social outlook. He was concerned that entering the political arena would jeopardize the university's
fragile economic situation.

Accordingly, during the Medicare crisis Macleod tried to remain
neutral in his public remarks. However, there was no doubt in the minds
of local professionals as to where he stood: he was the "Red Dean," the
government cat's-paw in the dispute. Early on he gave an interview to a
reporter from the *Toronto Star* in which he deplored the unwillingness
of the doctors to accept the government's promise to treat the profession fairly and to be bound by public opinion. This interview was ignored by the Saskatoon and Regina media. But after the *Saskatoon
Star-Phoenix* and the *Regina Leader-Post* carried full-page ads listing all
the doctors who were opposed to Medicare, identifying many of them
as teachers in the College of Medicine, Macleod responded; he regarded
the ads as an attempt to mislead the public into believing that his own
staff opposed his views. He authorized his old CCF friend Sandy Nicholson to use the *Star* interview in any way he wished.[23] The provincial
government promptly had it reprinted in the *Star-Phoenix*.

Macleod sent a memorandum to President Spinks on 28 June 1960
with his version of the event:

Re: the "threat to strike" signed by 130 doctors of this city with the
footnote stating that 86 of these are "teachers in the College of

Medicine." Of the 86 signers, 80 are part time and they represent 70% of the part time teachers in Saskatoon. Several have told me they regretted signing, but it seemed to them the wise thing to do.

My desire since last fall has been to avoid even the appearance of political partisanship, but rather to focus attention on the more careful use of terms and a breaking down of medical care proposals into the various basic issues. I thought it would be unwise to take part in any of the debates or panel discussions but assumed that in due course there would be opportunity for a carefully done newspaper interview. Weeks went by without any show of interest by our local people. For this reason, I welcomed the chance to talk with the very reasonable reporter of the Toronto *Star* on May 30.

Mr. Rose's report in the Toronto paper the following morning was brief and did not touch on the main themes. Yet I believe it served a purpose. Reports from medical and lay sources in the Maritimes, Quebec and Ontario suggest that it has been good for the reputation of our province and our university for discerning people elsewhere to know that the propaganda of the College of Physicians and Surgeons was not acceptable to everyone, and that some presumably responsible individuals could distinguish between the principles of a proposed plan and its modus operandi to be worked out by an advisory committee.

I regret the mode of sponsorship of the same report in the *Star-Phoenix* a week later, but must take full responsibility for it. It became clear that our paper would not carry either the Toronto news item or a story done by Canadian Press on instruction from its Toronto office. It was the doctors' ad which was the "last straw" and when Mr. Nicholson called me about it, I offered him the *Toronto Star* statement to use intact. I am deeply sorry if this publicity has embarrassed you in any way.[24]

An outraged Spinks informed Macleod that his actions had cost the university a great deal of financial support in the ongoing campaign to raise funds. He began to harass Macleod in a variety of ways. One was to forbid him to approve, without the president's consent, leaves of absence of longer than one week for department heads. Another related to the college's submission to the Advisory Committee on Medicare chaired by W.P. Thompson, which was critical of the university's role in supporting teaching and research in the College of Medicine. Spinks insisted that Macleod submit the brief to the Medical Committee of the Board of Governors. Macleod felt that Spinks had no right to make such a demand. He consulted Thompson, who apparently said, "If they ask you to change it, tell them to go to hell."[25] In any event, the brief was presented to the board on 10 January 1961. As Macleod recorded in his diary, "Knuckles rapped on account of (a) I didn't get the consent of the President and Board and (b) we specify deficiencies in teaching and research facilities at U of S." The brief was subsequently rewritten to Spinks's satisfaction, but the situation continued to deteriorate. Macleod was concerned that he was losing the autonomy he had achieved under Thompson. "The things I can do are about over," he wrote.[26]

But disengagement was not easy, for he had grown to love Saskatchewan. On 19 February 1961 he wrote: "wonderful sun and snow – bless Saskatchewan, but with rot in the medical profession." On his fifty-sixth birthday on 2 March, he decided to leave "in due course" after learning that the university board had cut his supplementary budget request, leaving Sam Wolfe's salary but no support for his office, and refusing to appoint an assistant dean. Two weeks later, on St Patrick's Day, he informed Spinks of his decision.

He formally submitted his resignation on 1 May 1961, with the date to be negotiated. His problems, however, were far from over. Spinks had now tied the budget of the medical college to the number of students registered. "Black Friday," was Macleod's response. "I think I'm played for a sucker – whether to shout and stamp or not."[27]

His relationships with the Saskatoon medical leadership continued to deteriorate. On 12 July he recorded the following, attributed to a senior physician in Saskatoon: "Scuttlebut via Badgley (SPM) and Traub (Radiology) – Douglas, Roth, Macleod and Osmond and Robertson will leave like rats from a sinking ship. The next Dean sure won't be a socialist. The strong president will seek a weak dean."[28]

That same month he received a letter from Dr Baltzan, the doyen of the Saskatoon doctors. Baltzan wrote "I regret that we muffed nine years we could have worked together. The reason is that you underrated the past, and that I perhaps resisted, overestimating the immediate future."

Macleod had also been serving on the board of the Centre for Community Studies (CCS), created in 1957 by the Saskatchewan government. The centre grew out of the report of the Royal Commission on agricultural and rural life (1955), which reported alarming changes in the conditions of agricultural life on the prairies. Bill Baker was the CCS director at that time. When Macleod and Baker approached Spinks to negotiate the position of the CCS on campus, the president was anything but enthusiastic. In a letter written during the summer of 1961, he objected to some of Macleod's remarks and suggested that some of them "were the same as the German views leading to communism and then Hitler and if sustained would lead to the loss of our medical centre in 20 years."[29]

Stunned, Macleod concluded that his task at the University of Saskatchewan was nearing an end.

Meanwhile, Sam Wolfe returned to Canada and was appointed to a full-time position as assistant professor in the Department of Social and Preventive Medicine. He was to develop a family practice research unit in association with other members of the department, including Robin Badgley, a sociologist; Bob Steele, an epidemiologist; Matt Dantow of public health; Hester Kernen, a public health nurse; and Edna Osborne, a social worker.

Unfortunately, when the matter of the family practice unit came before faculty, three department heads did not support it, and it failed. Macleod subsequently felt he had been remiss in not pushing the matter harder, and attributed the lack of support to the fact that the department heads were feeling insecure and did not wish to irritate their colleagues in private practice who were opposed to the idea.

On 25 September 1961 Macleod noted: "Spinks flays Sandy [Robertson] because he used his title and department in signing a letter to the paper. I argue that much of his medical care argument was not political but relevant to his subject matter. Spinks terminated the conversation by angrily declaring it distasteful – 'to be resumed another time' as he rose." Macleod wrote: "This is a little person with enormous hostility, an uncontrollable temper and dubious integrity."[30]

The straw that broke the camel's back was the decision of the College of Physicians and Surgeons of Saskatchewan to call for a withdrawal of services in the event of an impasse over the Medicare legislation that the government intended to bring in on 18 October. On 28 November, Macleod learned that the full-time clinicians group at the university had decided to endorse the CPSS decision. The following day he wrote to Spinks, asking to be relieved of his duties immediately.

On 2 February 1962, Macleod and Jessie left Saskatoon for good. Jessie had said of him that "he was incapable of recognizing danger." He agreed, and often reprimanded himself, writing, "my greatest error: to be able to skirmish with the gravest danger and not be stimulated to invoke emergency measures."[31] Even so, the Saskatoon years were marked by signal accomplishments, and he gave much more to Saskatchewan than he got.

Sam Wolfe resigned from his full-time position in the summer of 1962. The opposition from local doctors and lack of support from his university colleagues had led him to conclude that he would be unable to develop a family practice unit under the aegis of the Department of Social and Preventive Medicine. Sandy Robertson also left the university in 1962. Because of his views on how doctors should be paid, he had been immediately suspect in the local medical fraternity, who feared a change in health care organization and funding. Their opposition had prevented him from realizing a major part of his teaching plan, the organization of a family-practice unit allied to the teaching program. When the Medicare crisis erupted, he was vocal in support of the government and became the target of a campaign of vilification.

Robin Badgley became acting head of Social and Preventive Medicine. Badgley claimed to have received the assurance of Dean Begg, Macleod's successor, that Wolfe would receive a part-time appointment, but this never happened. Wolfe went on to develop the Saskatoon Community Clinic, a successful model of its kind. The other community clinics in Regina and Prince Albert survived the Medicare crisis but never attained the degree of excellence of Wolfe's model.

With Sandy Robertson's departure Macleod's dream of a unique Department of Social and Preventive Medicine died. In August 1962 Badgley resigned to join Robertson at the Milbank Fund. All were casualties of the Medicare battle. "Nevertheless," Macleod wrote, "a mark has been made! A standard writ in the sky!"

In retrospect, one may ask what the medical accreditation bodies (liaison survey committees) thought of Macleod's medical college and its curriculum.

The 1957 survey report suggested that in comparison with other medical schools, the Saskatoon program included too much didactic and formalized instruction in all four years; not enough student responsibility in the clinical team managing patients; and too much concern with extensive coverage of all aspects of medicine rather than with intensive study of selected instances of disease. The surveyors stressed the need for additional full-time faculty in both basic science and clinical departments, more personnel for the library, and executive assistance for the dean.

A second survey in 1965 concluded that there had been little change since the first survey and warned that the time had now come when remedying these persistent problems could no longer be ignored. The surveyors called for more adequate financial support and space for the faculty, increased research activity, executive assistance for the dean, and revitalization of the medical library. They found conflicting aims for the school among the faculty and suggested that objectives should be redefined. They noted that the curriculum had not been significantly changed since 1957.

A radical new curriculum designed to solve these problems was introduced in September 1968. The survey report of 1969 stated "this College of Medicine receives grossly inadequate support for the educational programs it has been required to undertake." In summary, the accreditors recognized that Macleod's ideas for medical education such as the Survey of Human Diseases and the preceptorships were ahead of his time. Their major criticism was for the university, which was never able to provide enough support for an adequate full time staff or support for the dean's office.

Macleod's students, colleagues, and friends all admired him greatly, and many letters and other documents to attest to this. (A selection of these can be found in appendix 7.) Two letters are quoted here.

The first letter is from James Graham, the honorary secretary of the Royal College of Physicians and Surgeons of Canada during the years that Macleod served on the college's council (1953–62): "Macleod was a good contributor to discussions, and he was articulate. He served on the committee that dealt with the approval of hospitals for advanced graduate training. He had a major role in presenting the brief from this committee to the Deans, who accepted it. His term on council coincided with his deanship in Saskatchewan and he got a good exposure to the College's problems in credentialing, examining and approving training sites. As a result, he could see both sides, the advantages of University participation in graduate medical education and training."

He continued, "Macleod was a gentlemanly, warm and friendly person with a superior intellect. He was a 'charmer.' He came to dinner one

Premier T.C. Douglas and Wendell, Saskatoon, 1961

night when my mother was also there. She considered him the most charming man she had met in a long time. He had remarkable energy and I don't think he ever functioned in 'low gear.' This was combined with an evident enthusiasm for what he was doing and devotion to his personal ideals. He was receptive to new ideas in medical education, articulate and possessed a fine sense of humour. He was an unforgettable man whom it was a privilege to know well and have as a friend and co-worker in the Royal College."[32]

At Macleod's farewell party on 3 January 1962, a long-time friend and close colleague, Allan A. Bailey, professor of medicine and neurology, spoke of Macleod as a delightful companion, magnanimous and generous:

Our Dean knew, as the great men of the ages have known, that there is a relation between the environment and the individual's state of health. Wendell could see that economic and social factors profoundly affect the health of many people ... He urged us to recognize the true meaning of a University – a place where scholars seek the truth about any subject and strive to anticipate the future ... He knew too that the zest for facts and new knowledge should not be a cold, calculating exercise. He recognized that the truth emerged where there was a proper balance of knowing and feeling ... In a real way he could lead any group to the frontier of medical science and speculate beyond. He always seemed ahead of us and some of us could never quite catch up. Wendell is best described by the following quote from Henry David Thoreau: "If a man does not keep pace with his companions, perhaps it is that he hears a different drummer. Let him step to the music which he hears, however measured or far away."

Chapter Six

The ACMC Years, 1962–1970

———□———

IN LEAVING SASKATCHEWAN, Macleod had to make a choice between contending opportunities. He had been invited to consider the
deanship at the American University of Beirut and the position of executive secretary of the newly reorganized Association of Canadian Medical
Colleges (ACMC). He took counsel with friends, and considered the potential effects of any decision on his family. Despite an invitation to visit
Beirut, he declined the offer and opted for the ACMC job.

He had in fact been appointed to the position on 15 June 1961, but
it was not secure. The ACMC had existed for twenty years as a special
committee of deans under the National Conference of Canadian Universities and Colleges (NCCUC), a body dominated by the university
presidents, who were not pleased to see an independent organization of
deans developing. They became more agitated when they discovered
that the ACMC intended to seek incorporation. Among the most dis-
pleased were Spinks of Saskatchewan and Hall of the University of
Western Ontario; they felt they had not been adequately informed of the
ACMC's intentions and feared that an independent ACMC might be in
competition with and harm the interests of the NCCUC.

Spinks informed Macleod flatly that the ACMC must relinquish its
pursuit of a charter. An impasse appeared inevitable, but cooler heads
eventually prevailed. Early in 1962 a compromise was reached: the
ACMC's new status would be recognized for the time being, and the situation would be reviewed in three years' time.

An account by Dr Douglas Waugh in the CMA *Journal* traces the ACMC's growth and development: "The creation of the ACMC was an almost serendipitous outcome of the Canadian Government's request to the country's medical schools to accelerate the program to double for one year the number of medical graduates to meet wartime requirements. Having met to consider this request, the deans decided that there were other matters in need of their collective attention. Late in 1942, Dean Alvin Mathers of Manitoba wrote to his fellow deans, 'Since there are many points constantly arising that would benefit from discussion among those interested in medical education, there should be a facility provided for this purpose.'"[1]

Mathers' initiative was supported by the CMA, and in April 1943 the deans met in Ottawa, and the thirteen delegates decided to form a national association. The purpose was not formally defined until the organization was incorporated in 1961. It was simply "to promote the advancement of medical education."

Before 1960 the ACMC functioned as a loosely knit but remarkably effective free-floating association of the country's medical deans. It was managed by its president, assisted by the secretary, each of whom held office for two years. At annual meetings, delegates and guests could be accommodated in a modest conference room on a university campus where they dealt with business in a day or, occasionally, a day and a half.

Postwar demands on the schools focused attention on the need for nationwide action and planning. A process of information exchange among the schools was inaugurated whereby the ACMC became the repository for data on student applications and admissions, student health and similar matters. In addition, the schools agreed to act collectively in their dealings with the federal government.

From its founding, the ACMC maintained close linkages with the CMA, the Royal College of Physicians and Surgeons of Canada (RCPSC), the National Conference of Canadian Universities and Colleges (forerunner of the Association of Universities and Colleges of Canada, or AUCC). These bonds became increasingly important as the fledgling ACMC began to exert its influence on preparations for a national health plan, the medical manpower needs arising from Canada's involvement in the Korean War, support for medical research, and similar matters that were too broad to be dealt with by individual schools.

By the late 1950s the business of the ACMC had become so voluminous that it could no longer be handled by a part-time president and secretary. In 1959 representatives of the ACMC, the Royal College, and the CMA met to consider organizing a Canadian medical education secretariat under the auspices of the ACMC.[2]

The search for an executive secretary resulted in Macleod's assuming the job at the beginning of 1962.

By his own admission Macleod lacked administrative skills, but with his considerable energy and charm he was able to create a multitude of links with important people and organizations in the field of medical education. When he took on the job, the organization was limited to one part-time employee with no permanent office or staff. He had to build from the ground up, and it was slow going. Until a Kellogg grant became available in April 1962, his resources were meagre, and there was even doubt that his own salary would be covered. The Kellogg grant also provided for a sociologist and a proper secretarial staff.

At that time concerns were being expressed about the inadequate number of doctors being produced by Canadian medical schools, and there was a pressing need for more information about trends in medical education and the career decisions of medical students. It was expected that the ACMC would perform a function similar to that of the Association of American Medical Colleges (AAMC) in dealing with these issues.

During the 1960s the ACMC developed strategies to adapt medical education to the changes in health care brought about by the national Medicare plan. An important part of this was the ACMC's definition of a clinical teaching unit as an instrument to assure that all patients in teaching hospitals were available for medical instruction. The ACMC also established a reputation as a leader in the study of the demographics of medical education in Canada. This data has become increasingly valuable as a planning resource, not only for medical educators, the CMA, the Royal College, and the College of Family Physicians of Canada (CFPC) but also for governments and granting agencies and as a source of information for the general public.

When Robin Badgley decided to leave the Department of Social and Preventive Medicine in Saskatoon to join Sandy Robertson at the Milbank Memorial Fund in 1962, Macleod was disappointed; he had looked forward to Badgley's assistance in consolidating the research arm of the ACMC. Still, he seized the opportunity when, through Robertson's influence, he himself became involved with the Milbank Fund as a member of its Technical Committee, which had responsibility for the fellowship program of the fund. The goal of the program was to find and foster leaders in medical education in Central and South America. Macleod's role involved frequent trips to New York, Washington, and South America to interview prospective fellows and write reports on their suitability.[3] He took great interest in this and thoroughly enjoyed meeting the interesting and intelligent people involved, though this was an arrangement that did not sit well with the board of the ACMC.

"I am very concerned, with reason, at your frequent absences," wrote Dr Harry Botterell, dean of medicine at Queen's University and president of the ACMC, on 24 December 1964. He reminded Macleod that he was "the servant of the Deans." Macleod defended his actions. He was forming links with important international bodies – the World Health Organization, the Milbank and Commonwealth Funds, the Pan American Health Organization – in concert with whom he participated in the planning of several important international meetings on medical education. He would play a pivotal role in organizing the Third World Congress on Medical Education, to take place in New Delhi in 1970. He believed his work with Milbank reflected favourably on Canada – to which John Evans, dean at McMaster, countered, "I couldn't disagree with you more."[4]

Macleod was also simultaneously sitting on the MacFarlane Committee, which was collecting data on medical education for the Royal Commission on Health Services (the Hall Commission). Chaired by J.A. MacFarlane, it included several eminent acting and former deans of Canadian medical colleges, among them R.C. Dickson, Harold Ettinger, Roger Dufresne, and J.F. McCreary, along with Macleod himself. The committee met frequently over a period of three years, and its seminal report, *Medical Education in Canada*, covered a broad range of issues in medical education.[5]

Macleod's membership on the committee came to haunt him, as he felt he was always behind in the work. Nevertheless, he made important contributions, writing the most important chapters of the report and editing the remainder. Among other things, the report recommended the expansion of Canada's medical pool through the establishment of new medical schools in the provinces that did not have them. Macleod subsequently played a part in the establishment of schools at Sherbrooke in Quebec, McMaster University in Hamilton, and Memorial University in St John's.[6]

The summary and conclusions of the MacFarlane report bear all the markings of Wendell Macleod: "There is a need for study of the best approach to community health requirements and the means by which these are to be met ... to study the nature of present day practice ... to evaluate our teaching as it evolves in the face of rapid change, and to introduce students to the practice of medicine in the community. We would welcome an experiment whereby, through an active outpatient department of a teaching hospital, arrangements could be made for the total care of a segment of the community limited in numbers to the requirements of teaching and research ... such a plan would require close relation to the department of social and community medicine of the school."[7]

He referred to the report as "a tremendous task, a real hallmark in Canadian History. It is really a magna carta of Canadian Medicine."[8] After a lengthy and difficult gestation, it was tabled in the House of Commons on 19 June 1964 with forty-one members of parliament present. Of the press conference that followed, Macleod had this to say: "No scrutiny of student projections nor of faculty supply – all we see is pie in the sky." A disappointing panel on the report was held at the CMA meeting in Vancouver five days later. Macleod felt they had "no sense of historical perspective nor understanding of social process, nor of logic."[9]

Early that year, after reading Solange Chaput-Rolland's *Dear Enemies*, a collection of letters on French-English relations, Macleod had copied a passage from the book into his diary: "From one ocean to the other, Canada seems to be frozen in an attitude which is rigid, conventional and desperately dull ... As opposed to us [the Americans] have numbers, money and power, but they also have audacity, and a taste for risk and adventure. We have lost these qualities, lulled by centuries of conformity and a sense of superiority. We have inherited not only our solemnity from our gloomy fathers of confederation ... but also from them a tendency toward the pedantic, the academic and the pompous." He asked, "Is this our medical education, too?"[10]

The executive and council meetings of the ACMC were now attended by representatives of Department of National Health and Welfare, the Medical Council of Canada, the CMA and the Royal College, the AUCC, the College of General Practice, and l'Association des Médecins du Langue Français du Canada, the latter reflecting Macleod's efforts to get francophones involved at every level. That and international education were a hallmark of Macleod's years at the ACMC.

Included in his ACMC mandate was the establishment of a program of national statistical studies in medical education. In 1964 he recruited David Fish, a University of Alberta graduate completing his doctorate at the London School of Economics. Fish effected major improvements in the collection and analysis of data on Canadian medical students passing through the system. Prior to this, the data had been sent to the AMA, where it was processed and published in the organization's journal alongside data from American schools. Under Fish, studies were also carried out on the career interests of medical students and how they changed over time. Costs of medical education were studied and later proved useful in improving the funding of medical schools. After two years the AUCC asked Fish to supervise their research as well. In the five years following his appointment, the ACMC published twenty-nine research reports on medical education in Canada.

Macleod played an important role in promoting the integration of Canadian health care organizations, evaluating their performance, dealing with accreditation standards, and examining criteria for entry into medical schools. Much of this work was done between 1965 and 1970 under the aegis of a supporting grant from Health and Welfare. In addition the department specifically requested that the ACMC examine medical school admission procedures in terms of validity and reliability, particularly with regard to the necessity for intensive pre-med preparation as a prelude to the intake and size of classes. The ACMC was also asked to evaluate the "multiple intake system," which provided an opportunity for able students to advance more rapidly and for less able students to fall back to the stream below without losing a year of studies. As well, the DHWC asked for studies aimed at assisting graduates into types of activity required by society to avoid over-enrolment or under-enrolment in certain medical fields.

Macleod was particularly concerned with the integration of Canadian health care organizations. He had long been troubled by the poor relationships between the medical profession and other health care professionals, especially nurses and opticians. An effective health care system, he believed, required close collaborations among all health disciplines. As ACMC executive director, he was in a position to effect change through his extensive links with various organizations. In October 1965 he orchestrated a meeting of representatives of the Canadian Dental Association (CDA), the Canadian Nurses Association (CNA), and the Canadian Council of Schools of Nursing (CCSN) to consider integrating their efforts. The ACMC and the CDA agreed to collaborate in a study of the overlap of applicants to dental and medical schools.

He also focused on an experimental approach to the problems of integration of the health team. He advocated that university medical schools create comprehensive care teams to provide services to a cross-section of the community, and to study how best to conserve personnel yet assure quality of service.

A recent study had indicated that the allied health professions were reluctant to come in under any kind of "medical umbrella," and progress proved to be slow, but Macleod persisted. He found enough interest among seven professional groups to warrant a meeting held under the rubric of a "commission on the health sciences" at the 1968 meeting of the AUCC. He contributed the insights he had gained on new approaches to the coordination of health workers through his work with the Milbank Memorial Fund and his site visits to the University of Kansas, Albert Einstein Medical College, and the University of Caldas in Colombia.

Health and Welfare also supported the evaluation of the performance of Canadian medical graduates. The ACMC carried out baseline studies on Canadian applicants for medicine and on the characteristics of medical students. These studies provided descriptions of "input" as a base for the evaluation of "output." Macleod and Fish were instrumental in encouraging medical faculties to help to appraise graduates' performance by keeping the necessary records to establish a national registry of all medical students. Eventually the registry extended to data on socio-economic factors, academic record, career choice, and patterns of migration. As measures of professional competence were developed and validated, it would be possible to use the student registry to correlate performance with a number of indices – type of graduate training, academic scores at various levels, and certain social, economic, and psychological data.

Things had improved enormously for Macleod at the ACMC since Fish's arrival, and they were further enhanced in 1966 when he hired Sheila Duff Waugh as administrative assistant. In the office Macleod knew all about everybody and was highly regarded by all. He always wanted to know what people were reading, and there were brief outbursts of celebration on almost any pretext.

However, these years were also overshadowed with personal worries. Jessie had not been well. She suffered from a cardiac problem that progressed to chronic congestive heart failure. Despite this, she kept working as a physician, a homemaker, and mother.

In February 1966 she died suddenly. At autopsy she was found to have a myxomatous mitral valve, which had resulted in severe mitral regurgitation. In the months following her death Macleod became depressed. Although Jessie had never been happy about his work schedule and his travels, she had played an important stabilizing role in his life and had helped raise Wendy and Peter. Macleod's response to her loss was to take on even more work – "far more work than he could do," as Sheila Duff Waugh later wrote.

A mutual friend at AUCC who "knew that Wendell was swamped" had introduced Waugh to Macleod. In a letter to the author on 10 February 2004, she wrote:

He knew of my close involvement with the NDP, and he said to me that he hoped I would never embarrass the ACMC, but if I did, he would defend me with all his resources. I was amazed by his expression of support for someone he hardly knew.

When I started in October, he introduced me to his desk, covered in foot-deep piles of unanswered mail, unread material, and unfilled forms, and asked me to do what I could. He then left for six weeks in India. He also left a bunch of bananas in his locked desk drawer, but that's another story. In his absence and with the help of other staff (notably David Fish) I was able to reduce the stacks to a moderate number of really challenging things that only Wendell could do. I learned a huge amount, and made any number of useful contacts, all of whom were eager to oblige when they heard I was working for Wendell. The universal affection and regard for him was a revelation.

Wendell was interested and worked hard on many things that interested him, but was a serious procrastinator if the matter at hand was less than captivating. I learned that if I wrote a letter for him that was just about acceptable, but not quite, it was irresistible; he would fix it up at once, and the job would be done. If it was too good, or not good enough, he would set it aside to work on himself, and it might never be done. It was a fine balance.[11]

Another of aspect of Macleod's work supported by Health and Welfare was the accreditation of Canadian medical schools. When he began with the ACMC this was done by the Liaison Committee on Medical Education (LCME), created by the American Association of Medical Colleges (AAMC) and the Committee on Medical Education of the American Medical Association. The ACMC had been concerned for years about the lack of Canadian input but felt that a wholly Canadian accreditation body would not be able to muster the necessary resources or command as much respect as the LCME. The ACMC did not wish to sever the existing relationship with the two American bodies; it agreed almost unanimously on the policy of maintaining close contact with American medical education through the existing mechanism for joint surveys of Canadian schools.

Macleod had been largely responsible for Canadian representatives being added to the survey teams and given a role in framing the recommendations after 1962. "The Canadian role in the survey process has become, each year, a more responsible one and this responsibility is likely to increase," he wrote in a report to Health and Welfare. "Nevertheless there would be value in having a Canadian Council for Accreditation in Medical Education representative of educational, professional and governmental bodies to coordinate standards in undergraduate, graduate and continuing medical education." At the ACMC meeting on 22 June 1967, such an organization was proposed by the CMA and eight other bodies. A steering committee was set up to look into developing a single program of accreditation for the continuum of medical education in Canada, and to establish better communication between the various organizations in Canada interested in the multiple problems of medical education at all levels.

The steering committee had its first meeting in September 1968 and agreed to begin by exploring ways of coordinating surveys (timing of surveys and standardization of survey forms). In December 1968 the LCME (AAMC-AMA-ACMC) and the Royal College of Physicians and Surgeons held the first simultaneous survey at the University of Western Ontario. It was successful, and both teams agreed to recommend to their parent organizations as many joint accreditations as possible. There are today four Canadians (out of a total of five members) on the LCME teams accrediting Canadian medical schools, and the team chairman or secretary is a Canadian. All reports now go to the ACMC as well as to the AAMC and AMA. The accreditation thus remains North American in scope, but more Canadian faculty members have an opportunity to contribute to the assessment and to broaden their own knowledge, and the ACMC can render a judgment based on its own scrutiny of the survey report.

A regular five-year cycle of accreditation has been agreed upon. Thus the LCME-ACMC surveys each medical school's total operations, while the RCPS surveys resident education in the hospitals of the same schools at the same time.

In 1967, with government retrenchment, the ACMC's federal funding was suddenly reduced. It was also the final year of the Kellogg grant, although the foundation had indicated that it would look favourably on an application for continued support. In his 1968 annual report, Macleod would deplore the fact that the ACMC was dependent on foreign granting agencies, there being no equivalent Canadian foundation.

When it came time to submit an application for renewal of the Kellogg grant, Macleod did not act, despite prodding from Fish and Waugh. Waugh recalls: "Eventually, David and I 'kidnapped' him on the way to work and took him to a motel on the Quebec side – no phone. David had all the required paper work for him. It was apparent that Wendell was seriously annoyed and angry, but being Wendell his response was to sit quietly and smile serenely and contribute nothing for about the first hour while David and I struggled with the application. Eventually he heaved a sigh, and pitched in with the contribution we needed from him. In the end the application was successful. I was never sure that he forgave us. It was an unforgettable day."[12]

In his role as executive secretary, Macleod was constantly on the move, planning and participating in the innumerable meetings of the many organizations with which he had created links. When he had first come to the ACMC, it was a conclave of the deans of medicine. Under his leadership it had become an important part of a much larger network that included the AUCC, CMA, RCPSC, CFPC, MRC, AAMC, and their licensing bodies. But eventually he began to realize that he could not continue to do justice to his many commitments. He decided he would retire in 1970.

On 6 January of that year he wrote in his diary, "At end of second evening dictating in office I encounter a crowd streaming from the National Arts Centre concert and I think, how crazy!" At the end of February he wrote: "*Apres le 30 Juin, mon ami demand, que fais tu Wendell? Response – j'attend Godot.*"[13]

When he retired in June, the deans hosted a superb dinner for him at the Cercle Universitaire. All along, Macleod's relationship with the deans had been generally excellent: cordial, admiring, and mutually respect-ful, despite occasional impatience with his chronic tardiness and his fre-quent travelling. Each dean spoke with eloquence about Macleod's role in his life. Macleod sat at the head of the table, beaming, tears flowing down his cheeks.[14]

Walter C. MacKenzie, president of the ACMC when Macleod stepped down, summed up Macleod's legacy in the ACMC *Newsletter*:

Wherever Macleod went, whether it was McGill, St. Louis, the Navy, Winnipeg or Saskatoon, he was a beloved teacher, a friend of students and an outstanding physician and consultant. He was one of the first to point out to us in this country that economic and social factors pro-foundly affect the health of many people … for those of us who have had the good fortune to know him personally, it is accepted that he is one of the best liked men we have all known. His general warmth of character and humility as a person have elicited a response of friendli-ness, and his own high ethical and moral standards have invariably been apparent in relation to his judgments. He is not one who feared to stand alone, if such a position appeared to him to be correct.

MacKenzie concluded, "Lest we pass by this distinguished col-league, able physician and scholar, and above all gentleman and friend we should record his tremendous dedication to the improvement of medical care, research and education on the Canadian scene and his re-markable achievement in this endeavour."[15]

———————

Shortly after his retirement, Macleod published an article entitled "Medicine's Responsibility to Society" based on a paper he had pre-sented at the First International Congress on Group Medicine in Win-nipeg, 27 April 1970. It provides penetrating insight into his views of what he thought the responsibility of medicine should be:

All of us here know too well the staggering differences in health status between the affluent countries and the less industrialized, so-called developing countries. What is less well appreciated is that simply to multiply the number of physicians and the amount of modern medical equipment in the distressed areas would make little difference in their

Retirement party at Le Cercle Universitaire, University of Ottawa, 1970.
Left to right: Dr R.B. Kerr, Dr Maurice McGregor, Wendell

tragic levels of morbidity and mortality. On the other hand, if we can improve the purchasing power of the family, achieve a good level of literacy, and mount effective programs of sanitary engineering and health education, the result in life expectancy and general fitness would be spectacular. The same remedy would apply to Canada and the USA where 30–40 per cent of the population lives in poverty.

Even the well-to-do middle class are unhappy about our medical system – although there is little hard evidence that the problems they complain about result in significant impairment of their health status. The real problem appears to be the limited availability of primary health care providers – be they doctors, nurses or other health care personnel, as well as the lack of continuity of care.

Manpower deficiencies are only part of the problem. Back of it lie deficiencies in planning and co-ordination, as well as inadequate in-centives for better geographic distribution of health care personnel, conservative medical traditions, methods of payment that discourage experimentation, lack of models of integrated comprehensive care in most teaching centres and narrow postgraduate training in hospitals.

In Canada today one half of practising doctors are specialists and the other half general practitioners. Of the graduates of Canadian medical schools in the decade ending in 1967, only twenty per cent have entered general practice.[16]

He went on to quote J.F. McCreary, a pediatrician and medical administrator writing in the *Canadian Journal of Public Health*: "I would assert that in most cities and rural communities in Canada a substantial proportion of people will not receive appropriate care until the physician relinquished to others some of his responsibilities for diagnosis and treatment."[17] He also quoted from Dr J. Bryant's *Health and the Developing World*, a survey of twenty countries carried out for the Rockefeller Foundation: "The insistence that only physicians can evaluate and treat the sick has had a paralysing effect on the design and implementation of health services and is one of the most serious obstacles to the effective use of limited health resources."[18] Macleod, McCreary, and Bryant all strongly advocated expanding the role of nurses and ancillary personnel as part of a unified health team.

Macleod talked about the principal determinants of the attitudes and behaviour of the physician, including the social setting in which he or she was born and raised, the attitudes and values of friends and teachers, and the social and economic atmosphere that informed and launched his or her professional career. Since the practitioner's attitude and actions are influenced by personal example, he wrote, we need to find leaders whose personal behaviour reveals a clear perception of the important issues of the day – courage to take a stand and rally their colleagues to constructive action. He argued that health centres should be a part of, not separate from, the community, that many students and young physicians were thwarted by old formats of individualistic, competitive private practice, and that society was asking medicine and its partners in the profession to recognize the social issues of the day and to press vigorously for their solution.

He listed some of the curious anomalies of modern medicine: an almost automatic denial of virtue in governments and government people; fixed ideas and practices in medical education; failure to use immigrant

physicians efficiently; toleration of intolerance, for example, by ophthal-
mologists against opticians; the blind veneration of the fee-for-service
method of remuneration in spite of increasing evidence of its inefficiency
in many situations; and lukewarm efforts to promote cooperation between
physicians, as in group practice and with the other health professions.

Finally, he summarized his basic beliefs on medicine's responsibility
to society: "Our first priority must be to assure adequate care for all individuals in our communities. The second priority – to do our utmost to
alleviate distress in the world community, affirming that medicine is
truly international."

Chapter Seven

The Milbank Memorial Fund, 1962–1971, and the Haiti Experience, 1971–1972

———□———

AFTER SANDY ROBERTSON left the University of Saskatchewan in 1962 to join the Milbank Memorial Fund in New York, he invited Macleod to become a member of Milbank's Technical Board to help establish a fellowship training program in the health sciences.[1] Candidates, principally from South America and the West Indies, would obtain five years' support from the Milbank Faculty Fellowship Program at $8,000 a year to study in established centres. In the period between 1963 and 1970, forty-five fellowships were awarded. It was a unique program that greatly strengthened the academic base of medicine in South and Central America and the West Indies.

Milbank wanted the fellows to have distinct objectives that would benefit their home universities. A report published in 1968 outlined the objectives of the program: to aid promising young educators in schools of medicine or related institutions in their professional development; to strengthen ties between medicine and the social sciences, between the medical profession and the community, and between the creative and preventive aspects of medicine; and to combine financial assistance with technical aid.[2]

Macleod joined the Technical Board on 14 May 1963. During his tenure he interviewed candidates throughout South America and met some of the leading medical people of Latin America. He was aided in this work by Robin Badgley, who had joined Robertson at the Milbank Fund in 1962, and by Per Stenslund from the Centre for Community Studies in Saskatoon. Macleod enjoyed his work on the committee, co-ordinating the training experiences of several different kinds of health care students. "What a destiny in these countries," he wrote.[3]

During this period he was involved in planning and coordinating a number of international meetings, including the 1963 Pan American Association of Medical Faculties in Cali, Colombia; the 1968 Caribbean Workshop in Barbados, which examined the health needs of four Caribbean countries as well as the role of the University of the West Indies in coordinating their programs; and the 1972 Pan American Conference on Medical Education in Toronto.

In 1970, having retired from the ACMC, he began looking around for something to do. Once again Sandy Robertson came to his aid. Robertson had now left Milbank and joined the Pan American Health Organization (PAHO). He asked Macleod what he'd like to do. Anything that didn't involve writing reports, Macleod replied.[4]

He was offered a short-term assignment to the State University of Medicine and Pharmacy in Haiti. He had travelled to Haiti in November 1968 on Milbank business, visiting with the dean of medicine, Raoul Pierre-Louis, and speaking with faculty and students of the school. He made another brief visit in September 1970, and by the end of the year decided to accept the Haiti position, although he had an offer from Queen's University in Kingston. Anxious about his ability to communicate in French, he sought advice from two Quebec colleagues, Roger Dufresne and Germaine Belisle at Sherbrooke. Belisle, a librarian, agreed to provide consulting services in Haiti.

Macleod's domestic arrangements in Ottawa were pretty much ad hoc, and he was having a terrible time cleaning up. "Approaching zero hour and same piles of paper on study couch and desk office," he lamented – "disastrous shortfall in packing and cleaning up."[5] Nevertheless, he made it to Haiti in January 1971 and stayed until June.

Haiti's University of Medicine and Pharmacy was in the midst of a building program for laboratories, a lecture hall, and a library funded by a loan from the Inter-American Development Bank. Macleod had been hired along with an American librarian, whose job was to advise the university on the establishment of a medical library and textbook program and to help find someone to train Haitians as librarians.

Macleod held meetings with department heads in an effort to revital-ize the Library Committee, which previously had never met more than once a year. He believed the committee's role should be to examine the objectives of the school to determine what books and journals should be ordered. It was a frustrating experience. Progress was slow, and it was difficult to get faculty involvement. In spite of impressive credentials, the American librarian was ineffectual and didn't last long. Macleod did manage to produce a list of textbooks and journals and got them or-dered; he also brought Germaine Belisle from Canada for a short con-sultation. There were problems over this with the dean, who wanted to import a librarian from France.

Macleod consulted widely with faculty and with members of the gov-ernment who were involved in health, and formulated plans to bring the school into the modern era. More important, in his eyes, were his plans for bringing a sense of social responsibility to the faculty and students.

By April 1971 he appeared to be making progress, but the issue of objectives for the school had still not been resolved. On 21 April, Pres-ident François Duvalier died and there was a cabinet shuffle. Max Adolph, the minister of health, was replaced by Alex Theard, a well-trained clinician who had been "Papa Doc Duvalier's" personal doc-tor. Theard, who was not an academic, had built a lucrative private practice, but Duvalier's family were grateful to him and asked how he would like to be rewarded. He asked for the post of minister of health. The previous minister was something of a nonentity, and had allowed himself to be manipulated by his employees. Macleod worked with Dean Pierre-Louis to prepare a brief for the new minister, but they found Theard "hopeless – he wriggles out of answering the most con-crete questions."[6]

Because of the disruption caused by Duvalier's death, Macleod was unable to complete his work in Haiti during his first 1971 visit. He wrote a report on what had occurred between January and June and sent it to the dean as a prelude to his official report, which he would send to PAHO later in the month.[7] He reiterated the terms under which he had come to Haiti and commented critically on what little had been achieved. He wanted some assurances about the future before deciding to return.

His early experience in Haiti is recorded in a letter he wrote to Dean Jean Pierre-Louis on 21 May 1971 summarizing the first six months of his term. It is a preview of the official report which he later sent to

PAHO. He outlined the nature of the assignment proposed to him by Sandy Robertson about one year previously to render advisory services to the dean of the Faculty of Medicine on planning for modernization of the curriculum, the equipping and using of the new facilities under construction, and the exposure of the students to the health problems and services of the community. He wrote: "In my exploratory visit of last September (1970) these appeared still to be the desired objectives."

In considering each of the three objectives, Macleod felt the library was the area where he had accomplished most. The discriminating selection of a modest number of books, periodicals, and reference works had been accomplished with the assistance of Germaine Belisle on a short-term contract. "I believe that his recommendations on library equipment, space and facilities and staff recruitment are sound and acknowledged by all." Macleod urged that action should be taken before the end of the month on a timetable for completion and opening of the library, the policy on library personnel (especially acquisition of a "biblio-technician" as recommended by Belisle); and the mode of utilization of the library by students. "Unless there is a radical change in the philosophy of teaching and learning on the part of both the professors and the students, with modernization of the curriculum, I am afraid you will soon have a collection of scantily used books and unused periodicals. This would lead rapidly to a reduction of acquisitions, of staff, and library services. The verdict of history would be that we embarked on badly timed, costly venture and you and I would be held responsible."

He next turned his attention to the laboratories:

The laboratories are nearly complete – but no lists of scientific apparatus have yet been made. In view of the catastrophe befalling the new equipment and exercises in physiology that occurred in 1962, what has been done to prevent a repetition of that collapse. Some expect my presence to be a safeguard. I have felt that you did not wish to seek or accept my advice. The advent of new laboratories has not stimulated or led to any discussion of the changing role of the basic sciences in medical education, relating exercises in the lab to the evolution of the curriculum. On my arrival in January I reported to you the suitability and probable availability of Dr Guy Lamarche, Head of Physiology at the University of Sherbrooke as a consultant who could advise on lab exercises and equipment and also stimulate fresh discussion on the integration of basic sciences into the total curriculum. Your disinterest in Lamarche, without other solutions to propose, has perplexed me greatly.

Under the heading "Social and Preventive Medicine," he wrote: "The meeting of March 19 served a useful purpose in reviewing the subject matter presented by each teacher. I am sure you were proud of the contribution being made by your new professors in anthropology, epidemiology and statistics. However from other standpoints the meeting was a disaster, and the Dean's surprise proposal of a community project was rejected. It was an example of how not to develop a new educational policy and promote cohesion in faculty. Nevertheless, I think a beginning has been made in utilizing the resources of the community in teaching."

On modernization of the curriculum. "Many features of the curriculum, particularly the examination system, retard the kind of learning I am sure you wish to take place. The results of the examination of 1960 for registration in Quebec revealed a pass rate of 23 per cent (compared with Argentina 47 per cent, Brazil 40 per cent and Mexico 19 per cent). Your system is in urgent need of scrutiny and reform. Education for the professions is most effective when the program of studies is based on clearly defined objectives which relate to the task of the physician in today's society." He then asked:

Frankly, do you have any serious reservations about engaging your faculty in discussion of your educational objectives?

I can assure you that at no time have I wished to impose "un programme exogène." It is your medical college. All I suggest is that, if you consider carefully what your objectives are, then I may be able to help you translate them into a curriculum which in every sense would be yours. I would like to know your feeling about this before I commit myself to return in September. If this letter appears brusque it is because I wish to be clear. Moreover, time is short. Let me assure you of my desire not to diminish your leadership but to strengthen it, and at the same time to lighten your burden.

When he returned to Haiti in September, he found that the minister had called for a meeting of the staff to consider the curriculum of the school, and Macleod was told to present his report within a week. "I'm ordered to produce a work whose value I doubt," he commented.[8] He considered it preposterous to create a curriculum without first examining the objectives of the school. Examining the existing curriculum of 1970–71, he found that 70 per cent of the first year was devoted to morphology, 30 per cent to physiology/biochemistry, and 0 per cent to the social sciences. In September he wrote: "Work to 4:00 A.M. on curriculum – then with François Dresse [of PAHO] to see Alix Theard for 1¼ hours – he [Dresse] is admirable, and not just because he liked my stuff."[9]

On November 5, Macleod visited with Minister Theard and found him friendly, "resigned," but determined to have a formal curriculum and timetable. Eight days later Macleod had completed part one of his curriculum to send to the minister; it was thirty-three pages long and of "dubious quality." By the end of the month the report was finished and in Theard's hand on 2 December. When he met the minister that day, Macleod found he had not only not read the report but was unaware that Macleod was leaving Haiti in five days. "Am overwhelmed again by preposterousness of the whole affair,"[10] Macleod wrote. (See appendix 3 for a summary of the report.)

He tried to persuade Theard that a consultant should be brought from France to advise further on the curriculum and other matters related to the university. Theard was not enthusiastic. On his way home from Haiti, Macleod stopped in Washington for a PAHO meeting. He contacted a French consultant, Dr J.J. Guilbert, and arranged for him to visit Haiti, indicating that he would be available for a final visit January 1972.

Macleod returned to Haiti on 26 January for a two-week visit and was able to arrange a meeting with Theard and Guilbert. "In his own incisive manner, drawing on his wide experience in Europe, Africa and the USA, Dr. Guilbert placed the argument for modern educational planning squarely on the line," Macleod wrote. "Most important he emphasized that changes in this direction were taking place in many countries, even in France. Whether this will dissuade those concerned in Haiti from attempting curricular change *before discussion* of the social role of the medical faculty, let alone any effort to define some educational objectives in useful terms, remains to be seen."[11]

Macleod was impressed with Guilbert's intervention, but it had little effect on Dr Theard, who had apparently learned nothing from either of them. The minister wanted a curriculum first and objectives later, if at all. On 7 February, the last day of Guilbert's visit, Macleod wrote: "I doubt the usefulness of any further work on my Haiti document."[12] In

Chapter Eight

The Last Years, 1972–2001

——□——

FOR THE FIRST TIME in his adult life, at the age of sixty-seven, Macleod was not regularly employed. Following his Haiti experience he continued on a number of educational and advisory jobs, including studies on health progress in Cuba and China and on immigration and health, as well as a variety of teaching assignments.

He took on the job of formally re-evaluating the functions of the Centretown Community Resource Centre (CCRC) for the federally funded Community Health Centre Study – the "Hastings Commission."

Founded in 1969 as the Ottawa Street Clinic, originally located in the YMCA, the CCRC's mandate was to provide basic medical care and community aid to the young, transient population of Ottawa. It had quickly evolved into a multi-service health, social, and legal service. In October 1971 it received a request from the Hastings Commission to participate in a study of community health centres. The project's objective was to research, with the help of an expert committee, the delivery of ambulatory health care on a community level through various forms of health centres.

The study included a request for information on seven issues: 1) What community needs ought to be satisfied? 2) How should community health centres relate to other community health and social service programs? 3) What should be the relative emphasis on community health or medical services, and what range of services should be provided? 4) What were the CCRC's views on sponsorship by community groups, and at what level of involvement? 5) What were the implications for manpower planning and training of existing personnel? 6) How should the programs be evaluated? 7) What were the political, financial, and organizational implications for any "restructuring" of services?

The request for information was widely distributed to university departments of social studies, medicine, nursing, and dentistry, and departments of social and preventive medicine. Macleod was asked to analyse the responses, some twenty-five in all, and comment on the recommendations. He eventually carried out a detailed analysis. Though he found it "a very stimulating experience," he was disappointed in the limited number of responses of the universities, particularly the departments of community and preventive medicine, and family practice. Half a dozen submissions were of high quality, but little more than half the reports he saw attempted to answer all or nearly all of the seven questions. He was shocked by several submissions, written by incumbents of responsible offices, which reflected superficiality, flippancy, antagonism toward the project, or misreading of its purpose.

Some of the divergent opinions reflected the characteristics of particular geographical settings, historical and cultural backgrounds, and the personalities and interests of leaders. Macleod did not hesitate to be subjective in his interpretation of the responses: "In general I have tried to ascertain the degree to which opinions expressed were based ... on evidence examined critically and on the level of appreciation of general theory concerning social change, the nature of profession, and the formation of public opinion."[1]

In a communication to the Hastings Commission on 27 March 1972, which he mailed from Madrid, he offered an analysis of social policy issues in the study: "The primary issues are political. Health care has become an electoral issue in which all political parties have interest, and since the parties are organized on a federal and provincial level, the struggles are more obvious at these levels. Political parties are the most efficiently organized consumer groups."

He asked, "Are health centres really centres of (economic) redistribution?" He answered the question by quoting the words of Prime Minister Trudeau: "I feel a just society would have to solve the problems of regional economic disparities, for instance, which means that people who live in regions which are underdeveloped have a claim against the whole of the society to be able to attain in some way average standards of welfare and growth, in order for the society to be just" (April 1968).

Macleod went on to analyse the federal government's actual responsibilities and involvement in the area of health care. He found that nearly all segments of the Canadian population benefited from federal involvement, but the one exception was "the transient Canadians, young and old, who are not eligible for Medicare because they have not met the residence requirements of the receiving province though they may meet the requirements of a municipality. This is the largest group of people not presently able to take advantage of Medicare and the Canada Assistance Plan."[2] This was precisely the group that community health organizations were most concerned about.

Although he continued to be involved in the CCRC, in 1973 Macleod took on a new project: he was offered a contract by the International Development Research Centre (IDRC) to review the health care literature on China and Cuba. The review was done in collaboration with Shahid Akhtar of the Information Sciences Division of the IDRC. The report on Cuba was completed that same year. Both it and the later one on China give interesting insights into the radical approaches taken by these countries in health care, and an assessment of their results illustrate valuable lessons for other developing countries. (See appendices 5 and 6.)

In August 1973 Macleod visited the Chinese embassy with Hazen Sise to obtain permission for a trip to China by the Norman Bethune Memorial Committee, of which both were founding members. The group had been planning the trip for several years and approval was granted almost immediately; they were off within a few days. Their chief objective was to visit the town where Bethune died and the place of his memorial.

Back in Canada, he continued his involvement with the Centretown Community Resource Centre (CCRC) and became a member of the Family Service Board (FSB), leading him to speculate, "Perhaps I am now getting into civic affairs." He reflected that Jessie would have been proud of him for doing so.[3] In 1975 he was elected chair of the CCRC. In a diary note dated 1986 he wrote that the appointments meant a great deal to him. Among his papers related to the clinic were notes probably made for a speech:

Not many doctors or nurses (and certainly not receptionists) had been in medical or nursing schools that had experienced the revolution in curriculum that included as one of its educational objectives to learn how to accommodate to difference – whether it was the rough clothes of a workman, the underwear that needed soap and water, or an illness due to a defective life style – don't blame the victim is now one of today's clichés. The goal of learning to live with difference today has to have wider applications. Our superpowers must learn it if we are to avoid crazy wars. Politicians need to learn it if we are to get through the work of parliaments, and the same is true in industry, educational institutions and even in health centres.

He recalled "the enormous amounts of goodwill that dominated the atmosphere" at the clinic: "Everyone was close to, or felt close to the people who came for help, and their need for help was often more visible than ... with our present clientele. In many doctors' offices they encountered disapproval, vindictive reactions and rejection. True, some had difficulty getting a bath. Each age and perhaps each domain of human effort produces its own orthodoxies, ideological rigidities, stereotypes – they fight to protect their own hypotheses. To some extent we are the victims of circumstances beyond the control of individuals." He concluded, "The ultimate goal is to serve people appropriately."

Though many years have passed since Macleod's involvement with the Centretown clinic, old-time members still remember him with affection. Betty Bergin joined the clinic in 1978 as a consultant-coordinator well after Macleod's tenure and was made executive director in 1979. She recalled seeing him from her office window at 100 Argyle, striding across the park, "a tall, lean, straight man who walked quickly and with purpose ... physically fit for his years":

I guess casual would describe the way he dressed ... he always looked distinguished, but not too business-like, which of course was in keeping with the philosophy of the centre and most of the people who worked there. Wendell really was special. He had an aura of wisdom and gentleness. Whatever the issue or concern, you just knew that he would understand to help to clarify things without laying his answers on you, and be supportive whatever the action decided on. All of this he did with the greatest respect, as if he were talking to someone his

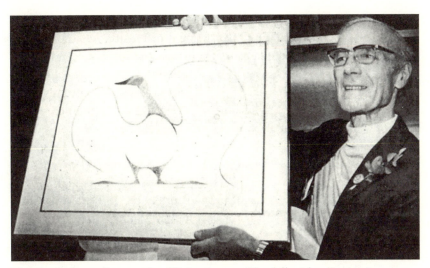

The Centretown Community Clinic presents Wendell with a Benjamin Chee Chee print in recognition of many years of distinguished service (Ottawa *Citizen*)

equal in experience and wisdom. Wendell seemed to be a natural communicator ... I'm sure he wasn't "putting on" how much he respected people and liked them. Sometimes I used to think we were his family. He was made an honorary member of the Board. We organized a party for him in 1982 when he was awarded the Order of Canada and presented him with a Benjamin Chee Chee print. I have very fond memories of him; a good and gentle person, a distinguished scholar, a wise man, a supportive friend, a doctor passionately concerned about the public welfare, a great Canadian.[4]

In 1975 another opportunity arose for Macleod: the planning of the Ninth International Congress on Health Education, to take place in Ottawa from 29 August to 3 September 1976. The conference theme was "Health Education and Health Policy in the Dynamics of Development." His task was to define the sub-themes around which the conference would be structured. He identified four: (1) health policy, social goals, and the dynamics of development as bases for health education; (2) trends in the organization of health care and their implication for health education; (3) the impact of health education on environmental risks and lifestyle modification; and (4) emerging challenges in health education.

The leading Canadian advocate of the conference was Michael Palko, a senior health educator in the Department of Health, who had held a similar position in Saskatchewan. There was friction between the two men, however, and by October 1975 Macleod was having serious misgivings about his involvement with the project. He decided to resign.

Meanwhile he had become a member of the task force on the development of new health immigration standards and guidelines for the federal government. He was involved with this group and its successor for five years. At his first meeting on 6 July 1975 he was impressed with the quality of the other board members. He decided to give the job his full attention and turned down an offer to lecture at the University of Manitoba, as well as an educational project with the Inuit. The immigration job would pay "God or Caesar," and that was enough. He admitted to himself: "Am already too busy and unable to cope."[5]

The task force turned out to be even more demanding than he had expected. It was charged with a revision of the basic rules governing immigration health, as well as the rules governing specific health problems. The existing laws and regulations, which went back to 1952, were badly in need of revision. The 1966 White Paper on Immigration pointed out that scientific and therapeutic advances had greatly reduced the risk carried by certain diseases and that the only persons who should be excluded from entry to Canada were those who would not be able to adapt to Canadian social and economic conditions or who posed a threat to the health and safety of Canadians.

The committee undertook an exhaustive review, creating a veritable medical textbook of immigration. In October 1976 Macleod wrote: "Am really inhibited by this task – whether to re-write a textbook or give bare bones."[6] As the work continued, he began to feel pressured; his writing slowed down, and he felt he must somehow get out from under "my overgrowth of tasks."[7]

In March 1977 he travelled to Winnipeg to fulfil a promise made to David Fish, his former research associate at the ACMC, to give a series of lectures to medical students at the University of Manitoba – "my account of medical education and care and institutional change over a 40–50 year period."[8]

Macleod titled his lectures "Social Epidemiology." From his years as a medical student at McGill he recalled three "ex cathedra" assertions by senior professors. First was from the dean of medicine: "The greatest conceptual advance in our time is the theory of focal infection." The

second was from the head of preventive medicine: "The best measure of
the effectiveness of a school health program is the number of pupils referred each year for tonsillectomy and adenoidectomy." The third was
from the professor of therapeutics: "Always remember medical care is a
privilege, not a right."

In that era, Macleod explained, "health needs" related to clinical
problems presented by individual patients. "People's expectations" and
questions of "accessibility to services" were simply not considered important. There were a few social workers and social scientists who were
interested, but they had little impact on medicine. There did not appear
to be a health system as such – the essential characteristics and structure
were virtually non-existent:

Fortunately in the last two decades we have had lessons from three directions that help us to view our western system in a wider perspective
and more objectively.

(1) Our system has not coped successfully with the health problems
of our population whose mortality and morbidity statistics resemble
those of a poor underdeveloped country (e.g., problems of tuberculosis, alcohol, drugs, violence and accidents).

(2) Other countries, especially European with western systems of
health care, have fewer infant and maternal deaths than Canada and
the USA.

(3) attempts to transplant our so-called system to poor countries
of Africa, Asia and Latin America have been failures.

Repeated WHO reports have shown a failure to produce an adequate number of doctors and nurses – less than 15% of the rural
population have any access to health services which seem to be re-
served mainly for the urban and wealthy population. Health services
modeled after our "western" system have simply failed to meet the
needs of the people.

Macleod quoted Peter Wilenski, a distinguished Australian physician,
diplomat, and international reformer, who analysed the western model of
health care and its relevance to developing countries in this way:

Medicine in industrialized countries is concentrated on personal health
and is firmly based on the individual doctor-patient relationship. This
is a system that developed naturally from that of the 19th century

when biomedical technology had little to offer, and the relief afforded the patient relied on his relationship with the doctor. As biomedical technology developed it was designed to be introduced into the individual doctor-patient transaction and was thus capital intensive and directed at curative rather than preventive medicine. It was concerned with diseases of little importance to developing countries, since western morbidity and mortality rates had fallen with increases in general standard of living, nutrition and sanitation. Unless a government can help a people to feed and clothe itself and acquire the basic necessities there is little that health planning and health programs can do.

What were the answers, Macleod asked. Some could be found in a new approach developed by WHO/UNICEF, which was to press for the speedy establishment of basic health services of a kind that could reach entire populations, especially the 80 per cent in rural areas. These services involved a major shift from a curative to an integrated curative-preventative approach, and a shift of focus from urban to rural populations and from privileged to underprivileged classes. Health or primary care workers were to be recruited and trained locally, selected by the community, with competence acquired for specific tasks that met the needs considered most urgent by the population being served. Finally, there must be a good deal of involvement of the local citizens in planning and managing the enterprise.

In 1978 Macleod went back to China as a member of a delegation of sixteen from the so-called Canada-China Friendship Societies. These "societies" had grown up in Canada over the previous fifteen years and were made up of persons who had come to admire the Chinese people and their accomplishments and believed that both rich and poor nations had much to gain from understanding what was going on in that huge country, its population then approaching one thousand million. The Friendship Societies were non-political, and their programs were for the most part educational in nature. The delegation was unique in several respects. Nine of the sixteen could communicate in Chinese; four were Canadian-Chinese. Three were born and brought up in missionary families in Szechuan Province, West China, and had lived there during their adult years. Macleod gave an account of the visit to China in a lecture at the Manitoba Health Sciences Centre in January 1979.

At two planning sessions in Toronto in July and August we recognized
the wide interests of our group, university and secondary schools,
engineering, computer science, community development, performing
arts, Asian studies, and two were medics. All of us were interested in
the swings of policy – the cultural revolution and the downfall of the
"gang of four" and now the "four modernizations." Since October
1976 anti foreignism has been replaced by renewed keen interest in
what the rest of the world has to offer (technical, economic, cultural
and even legal and political). Caution and suspicion have been replaced by extreme friendliness and openness, restrictions on movement
and travel have all but disappeared. We were all determined to find
out what had happened to the "cultural revolution" – what residue
could still be seen? Will the drive to modernize endanger the cultural
revolution's valuable features? Contrary to many reports in our media
we found that the basic positive goals of the cultural revolution and
the essential philosophy of Mao Tse Tung still enjoyed respect.

The body of the lecture consisted of a condensed history of modern
China, during the thirty years of the People's Republic of China (PRC).
Macleod felt that this might help to explain the present campaign for
modernization and also the drive for increasing contact with North
America and Europe:

First of all we should note the unique spirit and morale that characterized the 8'th route army in its long march of over 1000 miles in 1935
from south central China where it operated in an area completely sur-
rounded by the Japanese armies. The "long march" skirted the western mountains near Tibet in order to avoid Chiang Kai Shek's armies,
and later positioned itself to attack the Japanese from the rear. Along
the way they liberated hundreds of villages, transferring land from
landlords to peasants, helping the peasants with their farm work,
coaching them in self government and self-help, in new farming methods and in programs for literacy, and everywhere they paid for the
food they got instead of pillage and confiscation of crops which had
been the fate of the peasant farmer in the past. Along with this went
political education ... Through eight years of war against the Japanese,
the communist armies liberated a population of 100 million which
then supported them in three years of war with the Kuomintang.
Foreigners who worked in these communities in the early 50's were

amazed at the spirit, sense of unity, energy and accomplishment, in the liberated communities. Productivity was increased as never before. Naively, many thought that the revolution was won. If only they could increase productivity further there would be enough for all and the communist state would be achieved.

Macleod then brought the political history of China up to date. (That information is included in appendix 6.)[9]

Early in 1984, in Macleod's eightieth year, he began to have concerns about his memory, though he continued to enjoy excellent physical health. As a member of the Immigration Review Board, he noted his "lack of focus" during long meetings. He found he got his days mixed up, and he had some difficulty getting to specified places, but felt that he was still able to get by.[10] However, an unsettling meeting with his old friend and Montreal colleague, the distinguished neurologist Francis McNaughton, sharpened his concern when he found "no real communication" with McNaughton: "It was pathetic."[11]

In September he ruminated on the condition of T.C. Douglas, who had been injured by a bus and was given to flights of transient detachment. Moved by Douglas's condition, he addressed his own quandary of "how to die with dignity and even graciously."[12] A year later he was feeling even less confident about his ability to cope on his own, and friends were advising him to consider quarters designed for seniors. "I have considered the Unitarian residence," he commented. "Am sending donation."[13]

The major event of 1985 was his eightieth birthday and a splendid celebration attended by his friends and admirers. Held on Saturday, 27 April, at the Skyline Hotel in Ottawa, it was organized by his old friends John Last, Helen Mussallem, Sandy Robertson, and Sheila Duff Waugh. In attendance were Macleod's family, friends, and a Who's Who of Canadian epidemiology and medical education. Also present were Tommy Douglas and his wife, Irma; Kevin White, dean of Bethune College at York University, who presented him with a plaque from the students; and Agnes Benedickson, chancellor of Queen's University.

The dining room was draped in Macleod tartan bows and ribbons. Peter Macleod narrated a slide show on his father's life, and Sandy Robertson gave a speech that Macleod quoted appreciatively in his diary: "The Red Dean's apogee has finally occurred: he is rightfully being recognized

Thirtieth reunion, medical school, 1984, Dr D.J. Buchan, Wendell,
Dr Harold Sugarman

Grandson Kenneth John, Wendell, and son Peter, eightieth birthday
celebrations, Ottawa, 1985

for espousing equity in health for all, a principle now universally accepted."[14] Robertson praised Macleod's understanding of Third World needs, and commented on his remarkable abilities of networking, giving as an example the Fourth World Conference on Medical Education in Chicago in 1959: "When Wendell walked into the room filled with people, the sea of people separated – hands were stretched out in friendship from both sides of the aisle – he remembered everyone, when and where he had last met them, their wives and children, and he's still doing it."

There was an opportunity for people to recount their experiences with Macleod. These anecdotes were collected in a book that was subsequently presented to him. Ruth Horlick recounted the story of "Macleod's Woods," the forest of two-foot-high pines in President Murray Park in Saskatoon, and Louis Perinbam related an anecdote about the 1958 WUSC seminar, when there had been some concern that the Soviets might invade Yugoslavia. The question was whether to evacuate the students without delay. Perinbam and Dr Leddy had their say, and it was getting late when Macleod's opinion was sought. His response – "I never make any decisions at night" – dissolved the anxiety.[15]

Following the birthday celebration, Macleod wrote a long letter of appreciation to those who attended:

This is going to a variety of friends – the 150 who helped celebrate on April 27 my recent "over-maturity"; also those who could not attend but sent greetings, and others whose friendly seasonal notes have been appreciated but neglected by this still poorly organized person who begs your forgiveness.

A fat book of exceedingly generous messages, solicited without my knowledge, overwhelms me. I wonder how I shall ever live up to this pre-mortem mythology! Still, I interpret a tendency to the hyperbolic as due less to our inflationary times than to a genuine spirit of goodwill. Looking around the crowd at dinner I realized how much I owed to the values and example of those present and of others who receive this message. In fact, my best experiences have been due in large measure to the stimulus and support of others.

My entry into Decade #9 has stimulated reflection on past personal and world experience, also on the prospects for the future, particularly for our younger generation – in our own families, our country and our world. I would be out of character if I did not indulge, even on this occasion, in my usual brand of homiletics ("tedious, moralizing discourse"). The deteriorating world scene and the limited vision of much of the leadership in the so-called enlightened nation states concerns me deeply, and I am sure, you too. The pessimistic predictions of major historians seem justified by world events and trends – yet never before has so much goodwill, honest generosity and desire to serve been displayed so widely by people, their organizations and a few governments – witness the magnificent response recently to starvation in Africa and Asia. Witness also the mass movements decrying the use of military deterrents as not only old fashioned and futile but gravely destructive of economic resources. Surely we should strive to consolidate and extend that body of goodwill, enhancing it with the tolerance that includes patience "to live with difference" – whether it be social class, body odour, skin colour or ideology. And what about "righteous indignation"? Each decade, I must say I have become distrustful of it – my own and other people's. My psychologist brother, Robbie, recommended goodwill plus the "phenomenologic" approach, often to suspend judgment.

But back to generosity; even on a large scale, it is not enough. We need a long term blitz on the entire poverty complex – illiteracy, disease, superstition, low morale, hierarchical social structures, strife and swelling military budgets. Today, unfortunately, there is no model of socio-economic/political development suitable for universal application to Africa, Asia, Latin America and parts of Canada. Fortunately, however, out of world-wide analysis of various factors associated with success or failure, certain basic principles are emerging. For example, the order of priority to attain particular social as well as technical goals must vary according to local needs and perceptions; and animative participation by local people enhances not only productivity but also dignity, responsibility, self-reliance and creativity. Such concepts of the development process are held increasingly, I gather, by scholars in international studies, overseas leaders (also Dene and Inuit) and others in CUSO, WUSC, UNICEF, Society of Friends, parts of CIDA and similar circles – a combination of scientific method, including experimentation, along with compassion and education, often remarkably selfless.

Cynics assert the exchangeability of human nature and, therefore, of behaviour; Pavlov knew better, as Norman Bethune learned. Changing our conditioned reflexes is difficult and 100% success is rare. But if some "critical proportion" of a population, as after immunization, gets "near honours" in trying, then a vastly better society is likely. Nearly all of us can become "instruments of peace." So much for my half-baked sermon.[16]

In February 1987 Macleod was anticipating an important meeting of the Norman Bethune Foundation. He was in good spirits and had "a zest for putting NB on the map"[17] through a celebration of the hundredth anniversary of Bethune's birth and the fiftieth anniversary of his death. A conference was being planned at York University for March 10–12. Alas, two days before the conference he wrote: "The pen of the writing muse doesn't work – do not give any more lectures, papers, etc."[18]

His handwriting had become increasingly difficult to decipher. He referred to it as the "Brodie tremor," a feature of his mother's family. He was prescribed a beta blocker (metoprolol), and it helped, but when the medication was stopped, the effect was obvious. His diary notes include an almost illegible draft of a letter he was writing to a physician on behalf of the wife of an old patient who was afraid her husband might have cancer of the bowel. A short letter to his daughter, Wendy, took him three days to write.

In the mid-1980s he had been spending more and more of his time in Montreal with Jola Sise, the widow of his old friend Hazen Sise. In September 1986, he gave up his residence in Ottawa and moved in with her. Jola looked after him until he moved into a veterans home in Ottawa.

In 1989 he made his last trip to China. He was accompanied by Dr George Jaworski, an old friend. They went to Beijing via Finland and stayed a few days in Helsinki while Macleod prepared his speeches for the China visit. Jaworski noticed then that Macleod was showing signs of being mentally unwell, "but hardly so."[19]

In a letter to Dr Harvey Barkun, Macleod described "the most important event of '93": an invitation that fall to attend the centennial of the Sudbury Mine Mill and Smelter Workers Union in Sudbury (local 598). "Their tradition included a treasured contact with Dr. Norman Bethune as he crossed Canada in 1936 raising money for his blood transfusion unit in Madrid," Macleod wrote. "In Kirkland Lake he helped the Mine Mill Unionists to prepare a report on silicosis, which, he warned them, predisposed miners to tuberculosis." In preparing to honour Bethune, the union had contacted Mary Ellen Corcelli of Bethune Memorial House in Beaverton, who suggested writing to Macleod.[20] This

Wendell with statue of Norman Bethune, Guy and de Maisonneuve Streets, Montreal, 32 July 1989. (*Montreal Gazette*)

led to a memorable visit with union members and a recollection of his experience as a worker-teacher with Frontier College.

In 1993 he visited Saskatoon for the fortieth anniversary of the College of Medicine. He was his usual charming self but candidly admitted that he had no memory for past events. In an interview in 2004, his son Peter summarized his father's state:

Wendell and Dr George Jaworski in Tiananmen Square, Beijing, 1989

Wendell with Chinese children, probably in Beijing, 1989

I think that Wendell's final years were ones of progressive loss of memory and more and more dependence on Jola, and Jola was needing more and more respite. She would take him up to Ottawa and we'd keep him in our house. Sometimes Marg [Peter's wife] found him difficult to keep in the house. He would want to go for a walk and he would get lost. This happened several times and we had to go looking for him. On two occasions he was brought home by people who found him. It became too difficult for us to keep him in our house.

On at least two occasions he spent some time in Central Park Lodge, which was close to our home. He was fairly happy wherever he was, as long as he wasn't being restrained. He was physically very fit. Finally, when Jola was getting quite run down, she started asking us if we could find a place for him in the future, and we agreed. We put his name on a list for the Veterans' Hospital in Montreal. But Marg and I didn't like it, it was too institutional. The Rideau Perley Veterans' Home looked much nicer: people had their own rooms, there was a central dining area, and there were enclosed gardens where he could walk without supervision and no danger of him wandering off.

Rather quickly, his name came to the top of the list; we had only two days to bring him from Montreal. Jola agreed with some reluctance; she would have liked to have another month with Wendell, and it was hard on her. I don't think it bothered Wendell very much at all. The room he had was fairly large and there was space for his things, his photographs, family mementos and some furniture. Marg and I got to see him once a week, but it was hard on Jola. It was not so hard for us, as we no longer needed to be on standby when Jola needed help to cope with emergencies.

The staff loved him and went out of their way to keep him happy. He was a slow eater, sometimes finishing his breakfast by morning coffee, and they joked about this with him. We would often take him for a meal or go for a drive. He enjoyed the airport parkway. He would occasionally ask, "When are we going back to Montreal?" He developed phlebitis in 1998 and was put on anticoagulants until he began to fall. The geriatricians felt his falls were more dangerous than a pulmonary embolism and I agreed to stop them. His ankles were swelling and he was becoming breathless.[21]

Jola was not happy with Macleod being in the veterans home. It was "a disaster," as far as she was concerned: "Wendell was placed in a closed ward where most of the patients suffered from severe dementia. There was no common room, no place to walk or talk. The noise and chaos was not to be believed. All the patients could do was sit by themselves in their rooms. They were not taken for walks. Wendell's condition deteriorated by the month. He could not understand why he was there and begged to be allowed to go to Montreal."[22]

She was able to take him with her to her summer cottage in North Hero on Lake Champlain in Vermont for brief periods, "which of course was great." These holidays continued until the spring of 2001, when he was ninety-six:

I took him to North Hero at the beginning of June. It was a trying trip for him, long and hot and he was not in good shape. He did not sleep well the first night … the second night was even worse, he was coughing and miserable. We went down to have breakfast … he suddenly exclaimed, "What's happening?" and leaned over the table. He cried out once and was gone. I accuse myself for not having reacted faster and called for help, but perhaps it would have meant more prolonged misery. The emergency people arrived, but did not think they should try to revive him. Peter thinks he may have had another heart attack or a pulmonary embolism.

At first Jola struggled with feelings of guilt that she had not reacted quickly enough to save his life. In time, however, she came to realize that it was "a beautiful death."[23]

Chapter Nine

The Bethune Legacy

———□———

MACLEOD'S EFFORTS IN PUTTING Norman Bethune "on the map" by bringing his achievements to public attention played a large part in Canada's eventual recognition of the Bethune legacy. His work with the Bethune Memorial Committee, his visits to China, his role in organizing the 1979 conference on Bethune at McGill University, and the subsequent publication of *Norman Bethune: His Times and His Legacy* all helped to demonstrate Bethune's impact on Chinese and Canadian international and medical relations.

The two men first met at the Royal Victoria Hospital in Montreal in 1931 before Bethune left for St Louis. After his return to Montreal in 1934, he invited Macleod to join a study group on the unemployed – a "tremendous experience," Macleod later recalled.[1] Already attending meetings of the League for Social Reconstruction (LSR), an organization dedicated to fighting for social justice for workers, he saw this as an opportunity for greater involvement in social issues.

Bethune had a profound influence on Macleod that was to last throughout his life. Both were firm believers in the Social Gospel. Bethune's exhortation to link the Social Gospel to action was a motivating force for Macleod's ideas and actions in years to come, and he followed Bethune's activities with deep interest.

Bethune succumbed in 1939 to an infected wound while serving with the Communist armies in China. When word of his death reached

Montreal, Macleod chaired a memorial meeting attended by over a hundred of Bethune's friends and admirers at Windsor Hall on 20 December. Macleod later observed that on that same date in China, Mao Tse Tung's essay entitled "In memory of Dr. Norman Bethune" was being written at Mao's headquarters in the caves of Yenan. "In it Mao focused on Bethune's selflessness: 'With this spirit everyone can be very useful to the people. A man's ability may be great or small, but if he has this spirit, he is already noble minded and pure, a man of moral integrity and above vulgar interests, a man who is of value to the people.'"[2]

Hazen Sise, the Montreal architect who had worked with Bethune in the blood transfusion unit in Spain, also attended the memorial; it was he who subsequently organized the Bethune Memorial Committee and invited Macleod to join.

Macleod's diaries contain no further mention of Bethune or of the Memorial Committee for several decades. Then in his 1973 diary he recorded "two new stimuli, China and Norman Bethune."[3] A group consisting of Macleod, Hazen and Jola Sise, Paul and Mary Weill, Ross Robertson, and Bill Gibson had been planning a trip to China for several years, and when Macleod and Sise visited the Chinese Embassy in August to obtain permission, approval was at once granted.

Their chief objective was to visit the town, Huang-shih K'ou, in Hopei province, where Bethune had died, and the place of his memorial, the military cemetery at Shih-chia Chuang. Macleod found the tomb "impressive."[4] They also visited the University of Peking and a number of Chinese cities, and found themselves subjected to earnest lectures extolling the progress China had made under Mao. Jola Sise later said that she was sceptical about the Chinese claims, but Macleod appeared to have accepted them enthusiastically.[5]

The opening of Bethune College at York University on 26 January 1974 was a major event of that year for Macleod. He attended, staying in the suite of the master of the college. The college pub was called "Norman's," and the walls were decorated with blow-ups of photos Macleod had taken of Bethune around 1937. "It warms the cockles," Macleod wrote: "opening fabulous."[6] A Macleod scholarship later was established to honour students who showed exceptional interest in national and international affairs.

Hazen Sise's sudden death several weeks later on 19 February 1974 was deeply disturbing for Macleod. Sise had planned to write an account of his adventures with Bethune in Spain. The memorial commit-

Wendell at the Norman Bethune Memorial Site, Chu Ch'eng, Hope Province, China, 1973

tee had difficulty maintaining its organization after Sise's death. Macleod was asked to serve as chair but turned it down and the leadership passed to Paul and Mary Weill. Still, he shouldered much of the work, dealing with procedure, minutes, and programs, helping to define the group's objectives, and working with the Department of National Revenue to obtain tax-free status for the organization.

When a new biography of Bethune appeared from Toronto's New Press in 1974, Macleod was asked on short notice to introduce the author, Rod Stewart, at a meeting of the Osler Society.

He noted in his introduction that it had been twenty-two years since the publication of the previous book on Bethune, *The Scalpel, the Sword* by Ted Allan and Syd Gordon: "Allan had seen a good deal of Bethune in Spain and Gordon was slightly acquainted with him in Montreal," he recalled. "Both were very much the products of the postwar '20s and '30s – with their frustrations, idealistic impulses and often realist reactions – like Bethune. The book reflects those times – much gut feeling, much tribute – warmly admiring, inspiring and prophetic."[7] Though he believed *The Scalpel, the Sword* would remain a classic, he understood that some, like Stewart, would find it dated. A popular history teacher at the University of Toronto Schools, Stewart had been been intrigued and moved when he showed his senior students the National Film Board's documentary film on Bethune. He had swiftly embarked on two years of full-time research on unravelling the Bethune story.

Macleod reminisced briefly about working closely with Bethune, unsuccessfully testing oleothorax, then getting to know him better "in the darkest days of the Depression of the '30s." Macleod felt that

Beth had discovered painfully that the social and economic aspects of society were frustrating his surgical efforts on behalf of the tuberculosis. To discuss this and perhaps to do something about it, Beth drew around him a group, mostly doctors, nurses, dentists and pharmacists – to consider, in the light of experience in other countries, how Quebec might provide essential medical care for its tens of thousands of unemployed and poor. It was an intimate group that had the privilege of witnessing Beth's transformation from a man who had come to realize his own ignorance of society, and indeed ignorance of himself, to become a person of social conviction who would become committed to social action. Some of us regard that experience from early 1935 until he left for Spain in the fall of 1936 as among the most precious experiences of our lives.

Macleod was not uncritical in his praise of Stewart's book: "Some felt that it did not do full justice to the process by which the intellectual man of action was transformed into the devout communist, later to be singled out as a model for emulation by the leader of the nation that is not only the world's largest, but the world's oldest continuous civilization, but also the nation that wins the prize for its unique victories over communicable disease, most natural disasters, famine, poverty, illiteracy and unemployment – all without inflation or debt. Some of us with a strong social bias would like to have seen more tribute to the PRC – but an historian has to limit the scope of his focus."[8]

The following year Libbie Park, a member of Bethune's study group in Montreal in 1935–36, contacted Macleod about writing an essay on Bethune's Montreal years. In October he met with her and publisher James Lorimer in Toronto. Lorimer encouraged them to pursue the project. Stanley Ryerson, who had also been a member of the Montreal group, agreed to join them in it. Park suggested that Francis McNaughton and Yetta Shister might also contribute. Macleod made a note to himself: "Don't mention Beth spending his bride's fortune on the honeymoon."[9]

In February 1977 he spoke about Bethune to medical students at Queen's University in Kingston, Ontario, and discussed overseas aid for the Third World. He commented in his diary: "Basically, I lack enthusiasm for work overseas intended to 'do good' rather than to learn from the people."[10] He accepted three additional speaking engagements for later in February and March, speaking to a group about health care in China on 24 February and to McGill graduates in Montreal on 5 March, and, at the request of David Fish, delivering a lecture series on changes in medical education and care at the University of Manitoba on 11 March. Of the latter, he wrote, "I can't say how good it was," but nonetheless he returned to Ottawa "feeling carefree and grateful."[11]

On 27 March he was in Montreal consulting on the Bethune project with Libbie and Frank Park and Yetta Shister, the widow of Hy Shister, another member of the original Montreal group. Although there were problems with Yetta, who did not want her late husband's name included in the manuscript, "We are encouraged," Macleod wrote, "even enthusiastic."[12]

By February 1978 he was chafing under a looming deadline. He would rather "concentrate on French language and letters," he mused, "have fun in Spanish, Polish, even German (even though no useful outcomes), and more time with friends."[13] Libbie Park was urging him to "get more anecdotes and stop editorializing!"[14] On 13 March he had fourteen days left to finish his part of the manuscript and send it to his co-authors and Jim Lorimer. When he did get it done, "elated by freedom again,"[15] he thought it was one of his best pieces of writing.

Lorimer turned the manuscript over to freelance editor Ingrid Cook. At 2:10 A.M. on 21 July Macleod finished reading Cook's edited version of "my penultimate draft – caused deep pain from violence done to the

1937–38 period of the group and omission of the Pavlov impact." He had finished his manuscript with a note on the group in 1937–38; Cook wanted only Libbie Park's few paragraphs on this period. He felt there were serious gaps, notably the link with Spain and China, and the origins of Bethune's beliefs.

In August and September 1978 he made a second trip to China as part of a delegation of sixteen people from five Canada-China Friendship Societies in Ontario. The members believed that rich and poor nations alike had much to gain from understanding what was going on in that huge nation, its population now approaching a billion. Macleod's delegation was unusual in that nine of the sixteen could speak some Chinese. (See chapter 8).

The group spent time in Beijing where, in addition to discussing friendship matters with their hosts, they spoke with senior government officials about state economic planning, foreign policy, and the performing arts. In Shanghai they discussed the legal system and the press. They asked for a week in Szechuan and got eight days, then visited Chengtu, Chungking, and the village of Jinsou. They spent two evenings in Kunming interviewing refugees from Viet Nam. In all the cities they visited, most evenings included entertainment: opera, ballad singers, song and dance groups. In Shanghai they attended a symphony concert, the ballet school and an evening of acrobatics. On several occasions they spoke with the performers themselves.[16]

In October 1978, after two years' gestation, *Bethune: The Montreal Years* was in press. The book was launched at a festive lunch in Toronto on 12 October. Unfortunately, no copies were available; a wrench had literally fallen into the press and damaged it! It was not until 23 October that Macleod was able to pick up two copies in Montreal. Early in November he embarked on a book promotion tour that took him from Halifax to Vancouver.

On 26 March 1979 a consultative committee of the Canada-China Friendship Society met at the home of Dr Maurice McGregor to consider the possibility of a major conference on Bethune to be held at McGill University. Once again Macleod jumped in with both feet and hands. The project was to consume much of his time and energy for the next three years, well beyond the actual conference, which was scheduled to open in November.

"Sleepless on account of problems with conference," he complained in July. "I am slow in writing letters to prospective donors. There is no secretarial help nor volunteers to put posters in tubes for mailing."[17] As of 26 July there was "not a cent in except for Libbie Park's donation." On 2 August he recorded that "for the first time am really blue about going to work re: conference finances." The Muttart Foundation had turned him down, as had the Hannah Foundation. "Why did the Hannah reject?" he wondered. "Was the conference not sufficiently historical? Did they object to the budget? to the Montreal setting and considerable Quebec emphasis? to Bethune? to me (the so-called Red Dean)? Is it the old McCarthy mood still in Toronto medicine?"[18]

He countered with some advice to himself: "So Wendell keep cool – don't cancel conference – maintain dignity, but consider letters and seek financial aid from liberally disposed medics." He felt this was important in order to "avoid the label of chauvinism for the entire profession and from labour organizations."[19] By 9 October there had been only three registrations, but promises of funding were beginning to appear, including the prospect of a sizeable grant from the Office of the Secretary of State.

And in spite of Macleod's forebodings, the Bethune Conference was a success. Mary Weill opened the proceedings on 15 November 1979. Macleod later wrote: "I hear less than half the papers. I revel in Marian Scott and Louis Muhlstock. Mayor Drapeau held a charming reception at the Hotel de Ville. November 16th was the highlight for many. This day [belongs to] Terry Copps, the historian from Sir Wilfrid Laurier University, Libbie Park, and Madeleine Parent. On the 17th there was a robust Quebec session ... 'Beyond controversy in health care ... the Quebec experiment.'" He had "extravagant praise for our women – Libbie Park, Marian Scott and Madeleine Parent."[20]

The conference ended on 19 November. Preliminary accounts showed a deficit of $10,000. Macleod was deeply concerned and dreaded the thought of having to engage in more fund-raising. Subsequent tallies in March 1980 showed the final deficit to be a more manageable $5,260.

His major concerns in 1981 were to raise funds to cover the deficit, to collect and edit the presentations from the conference, and to assure their publication. He wrote many letters and made countless personal appeals for support. He enlisted the help of his old ACMC associate John Evans in an attempt to influence the secretary of state, Francis Fox, "who has a slush fund,"[21] to provide some support. The effort failed. The Bronfman Foundation agreed to match a $2,500 contribution, which the Bethune Committee borrowed from the bank. That money and support from the Canadian Public Health Association were dedicated to the production of the report, *Norman Bethune: His Times and His Legacy*. A major grant from CIDA helped wipe out the deficit.

Macleod worked with David Shephard on revising and editing the manuscripts and undertook to collect illustrations for the book. By the end of the year the work was virtually complete, but publication was delayed until, once again, funding could be found. A welcome break-through came when the Hannah Foundation agreed to match the Bronf-man and Bethune Committee funds. "That will give you something to work with," wrote Jack Neilson of the Hannah Foundation. "*Gruss Gott!*" Macleod responded.[22] Publication was assured.

On 2 March 1982 Macleod noted triumphantly: "Enter 78th year! ... *La vie est bonne!* ... Despite Ronald Reagan and world scene, am glad to be alive." Some problems remained, however. On March 29 he wrote that the promotional flyer for the book was "disastrous – it has not been proof-read – the back cover has the name Norman Bethune in black instead of red which makes the too intense pink completely irrel-evant plus three major errors in French." He felt badly that he had not proofed the flyer and attributed the lapse to his "slowness in the weeks preceding production."[23]

In April the final proofs arrived from David Shephard, and Macleod and historian Andrée Lévesque reviewed them. Macleod, no doubt ex-amining the galleys closely after the flyer fiasco, discovered "lots of errors."[24] But by the time *Norman Bethune: His Times and His Legacy* finally emerged on 6 May, he exulted: "The book looks great."[25] David Shephard and Andrée Lévesque were credited as editors for the Bethune Foundation, and the Canadian Public Health Association was the publisher.

A launch was organized for 14 May in Montreal. But again a span-ner was thrown into the works: Macleod learned that only twenty copies would be available for the launch, "and I don't know who all are coming. No invitations have gone out to Rod Stewart or to the Mon-trealers – but good news – many flyers have been sent out." His friend Pierre Delva said they would just have to sell the books after the launch.[26]

For Macleod the event was "exciting in many ways" –

the locale – the 30th floor of La Banque Nationale at 500 Place D'Armes (site of a boys' school founded 296 years ago) with fascinating views of Montreal, *la fleuve*, and the Adirondacks and Green Mountains. There were only 70–75 present on account of the blue skies and spring warmth and the exodus of our social class to the countryside. Alas, to have Monique Bégin, admired Minister of Health, we changed the date from a Monday to a Friday; finally she cancelled but sent a nice wire. Present, to warm our hearts, were Marian Scott, Jessie Scriver, Stanley Ryerson, and Francis McNaughton. Marcel Knecht and Peter Delva handled the ceremonials admirably. Dr. Verdy demanded a retranslation of Liu Chinghua's pro-ambassadorial speech into French. It was done by a tri-lingual Quebecois (Jewish, I think, and admirably). The dinner-buffet that followed was at the wonderful Delva's home. The launching of the book has given me an enormous feeling of release and of a free life beginning (although there is a lot to do about mailing and steps to provide awareness of the book across the country.[27]

Several contributors in the section on Bethune's Canada years dealt with socio-economic conditions in Canada, while the final section on Bethune's legacy included a round-table discussion of health care in Quebec in the post-Bethune years. It was a wonderful testimony to a great Canadian, full of insightful analyses of the man and his career.

Ted Allan's essay, "With Norman Bethune in Spain," touched on the hero aspect. Allan wrote that Bethune was unhappy in Spain. Having visited Russia, he considered communists to be the most committed of anti-fascists, but not all the Spanish who Bethune worked with matched this image. Some were not totally committed to the cause, he thought, and some made him feel that they didn't really need him. It was in China that he met the communists who fitted his anti-fascist model, and their effect was to transform him, to the point that he become the first foreigner to be revered by the Chinese as a hero. The thought that Bethune, a man with failings and weaknesses, could become a hero suggested to Ted Allan that "each one of us, too, can become a hero."[28]

A particularly interesting contribution is Maurice McGregor's "The Bethune Legend: Norman Bethune as Hero." McGregor considers the dimensions of the Bethune legend in China even after the passage of forty years now demands an explanation: "For Mao Zedong, particularly, Bethune was a local good Samaritan who taught the Chinese people the lesson of self-reliance, service and internationalism; values exemplified in Bethune that were of especial significance in modern

China are responsibility and devotion to others without thought of self. Bethune, who thought of himself as one of the Chinese, is more of a Chinese than a Canadian hero; and the Bethune legend tells us more of modern China than of Bethune himself. The Bethune legend tells us that modern China has chosen for two of its principal goals democratic and egalitarian service to the people and a spirit of internationalism."[29]

Macleod himself summarized the essence of the conference in a piece entitled "Reflections." What would Bethune have made of what occurred during these three days?

Bethune would notice, no doubt, great gaps in our accomplishments. We have yet to learn how to distribute health personnel geographically and by social class in order to serve all groups fairly. Part of our population still has the dismal health and social record of an underdeveloped country. We have made only a slight dent in the problem of faulty lifestyles that cause misery, inefficiency, and premature disability and death. Even more sad is the widespread apathy in these matters ... Looking at our society as a whole, beyond the health care system ... I think he would explode! He would recognize too much of what had revolted him before: our selfish preoccupation; our indifference to gross disparities and indignities at home and abroad; and our narrow nationalism and failure in so many ways to profit from the experience of two world wars and other conflicts. He would point the finger at an economic and social structure that leads inevitably toward self destruction. I doubt that he would spend much time on conferences unless they led to action. Bethune has left us a legacy. The challenge is in our court.[30]

In 1983 Macleod received a letter from a grade-six Toronto schoolgirl named Vivian Schwartz asking some questions about Bethune. He answered her at length, and in the years that followed, continued to write and speak about Bethune.

Vivian Schwartz asked about Bethune: "What kind of man was he? What did he like to do when he wasn't working? Can you tell me about the art program that he ran in Montreal for children?" Macleod's response was typically late; he had lost her letter while clearing away his files on the living room floor while trying to take advantage of a bargain in rug cleaning! His reply was written by hand on Saturday noon, 28

May 1983, at an Italian restaurant in Kingston, where he had been attending convocation. His answers represent a distillation of his deep emotional attachment to Bethune.

(1) What sort of man did I find Norman Bethune? – fascinating, inspiring, again and again a challenge to me to overcome my own shortcomings. I was indecisive; he was quick to move from the idea to action. My ideas were often ordinary – the usual, he always looked for a better idea and a better way to act on it. If a thing or a job had been done the same way for a long time he would assume that it probably needed improving. He thought that complacency was not only dull – it was often damaging to the best parts of a person, sometimes dangerous!

Another point: Norman B had so many parts in his own personality or make-up. Most of these reflected as in a mirror, his many types of experience. As a boy he helped and observed the men who worked in the woods, in the sawmill and on the boats in the St. Lawrence river and the Great Lakes. After finishing high school he spent two whole fall and winter seasons in the lumber camps. He was a soldier in World War 1, was wounded in one of its worst battles, where he was a stretcher bearer. On the other hand, he and his brother and sister, all small kids, used to carry presents of food and comfort from their mother to sick and elderly patients in their town. His father also was kindly, a minister who tried to do good things. So, young Norman grew up to be very generous to people in need, as when he gave his overcoat to a poor man on a Montreal street in winter, cold and hungry.

As a result he had a range of ways of doing things – gentle and tender, but also on occasion rough or crude! This sometimes upset people brought up in a very proper manner, never exposed to poverty and what it can do to people.

A final quality I admired: his great curiosity about so many things – how they came to be; how they worked. He would see for himself, or read books about them. This leads into your second question.

His favorite pastime was discussion and argument. Sometimes he was dogmatic, laying down the law; sometimes arrogant, even unpleasant. In my own experience with him at the Royal Victoria Hospital in Montreal and later in his "health study group" he was always patient, tolerant, and eager to help each of us make a good contribution to our task: to work out a plan for doctors' and nurses' services (and many

others) that would help everybody, the poor as well as the rich, the
people of small villages as well as those of big cities.

It was in the years 1932–36, the second half of his eight years in
Montreal, that his interests moved toward "social goals," that is to
put most of his energy into two causes. The first was to urge his own
profession to organize its own work so that serious disease could be
prevented (whenever possible), rather than treating mostly the late
stages of the killing diseases. The second cause was to urge society
to work towards getting rid of poverty and all its effects – unemployment, wretched housing, and for thousands of people during the Great
Depression of the 1930's, simply enough food to eat. This brings us
to your third question, what he did on Saturday mornings in 1936,
which others carried on later.

(3) Norman Bethune and the Children's' Creative Art Centre (or
Art School). Bethune's surgical work at the French hospital (Sacre
Coeur, 1933–36), gave him more time for his favorite hobby, painting,
as well as for the social goals just mentioned. For him, painting was
not just fun; rather, it should help the painter to express his feelings,
develop his imagination, even change his life in important ways. In
fact Bethune thought that the same thing could happen to the poet,
the musician, and even to the person who considers his work an art,
and himself in a sense, an artist – as Bethune looked on the true artist
as a creative spirit of life working in the soul of man.

Norman B invited a dozen children, mostly from the unemployed
or poor people to come with him on Saturday morning for a trip to
such places as a shopping centre, a factory, or a busy street, people
coming to church or waiting for a bus – then going to his apartment,
where he placed large sheets of paper on the floor, along with finger
paints, crayons etc. He then asked the kids to paint what they saw,
letting their feelings show in colors, the lines, the spaces – in any way
they wished. Artist friends helped him. Sometimes they started with a
discussion of what they saw and how they felt. Amazingly their paintings revealed all kinds of feelings – anger, sadness, feeling crowded or
lonely, frightened or a mixture. Then they would all discuss the different paintings. The whole thing made everybody think about life and
people, as well as learning painting.[31]

In 1984 Bethune College at York University recognized Macleod's role
in establishing the college with the annual Wendell Macleod Award. In

Wendell and Margaret Laurence at the dedication of Norman Bethune College houses in their honour, York University, 1983.

a memorandum to David Lumsden, master of Bethune College, dated 14 May 1984, Macleod expressed some of his thoughts about Bethune and the intent of the award:

We should avoid excessive or exclusive reference to him as "the great humanitarian" or "the surgeon who brought blood to the wounded." True, always a man of action, he devoted himself passionately and with ingenuity to whatever he did, and he had deep compassion for those he pitied. But his perception grew with new experience – personal and professional, then social and international, and so did his priorities and sense of urgency. He went to Spain and China primarily to defeat Fascism, Nazism and military dictatorship, to prevent devastating European and then World War, in order to build a new and democratic society; one that would truly serve the people. The new society should provide more than health. It should ensure security, decent living and a chance for all to enjoy some measure of his own "lust for life." To overlook this aspect of Bethune's evolution in vision and motivation is to emasculate him; to classify him as one of the most energetic of "do gooders."

As the Chinese struggled to repel the invader and build their new society they recognized the rare qualities of the foreigner that had raised the morale of both soldiers and the people, both young and old. These were his spirit of internationalism, his great sense of responsibility toward his work and constant attention to improving his technique and his utter devotion to others, without thought of self. Hence the hero status of Bethune, still unique for a foreigner and in the hearts of the Chinese, second only to Chou en Lai.

Macleod was preoccupied throughout the year with the future of the Bethune foundation. Feeling that Pierre Delva, the foundation's president, was unrealistic in his ideas, he worked intermittently on a new set of objectives for the foundation, feeling that its survival would depend on a focus on real issues. He considered concentrating on socio-economic development in the Third World through an experimental approach to social structures and goals. One possibility he considered was of trying to enlist former CUSO volunteers who had been exposed to Third World problems and had gone on to specialized careers in economics and political science. But by the end of the year no real agenda had emerged.

In July 1989 Macleod was eighty-four years old and suffering from moderate cognitive impairment when he gave an interview to Alan Hustak, a reporter for the *Montreal Gazette*. It was ostensibly about the delay in the production of the film *Bethune: The Making of a Hero*, jointly financed by the CBC and the Chinese government. Macleod waxed enthusiastic about Bethune and defended his sometimes rude and autocratic behaviour, dispelling the common Montreal myth that Bethune was loved by millions but was not himself a lovable man.[32] The publication of the interview was followed a week later by an article, also in the *Gazette*, by Ruth Wisse of McGill, who suggested that Macleod, like many well-meaning Canadians, had been duped by what was in effect a communist conspiracy:

The Communist Party of the 1930s was on the lookout for precisely this kind of recruit – a highly competent, educated, and socially prominent individual who was drawn to the party by free-floating idealism, but who would then be exploited for its practical political ends ... Norman Bethune proved to be the greatest catch the CP ever made ... In fact Bethune was actively spreading a carefully constructed disinformation campaign designed to conceal the largest slave labour and extermination system the world had ever known ... Bethune admitted the moral ambiguity of communism to his audiences and then invited them to brush all scruples aside. When Bethune died in 1939 he was declared a hero by Mao Zedong, who saw in him a superb tool of posthumous propaganda.[33]

Helen Mussallem, Macleod's frequent companion in the years following Jessie's death, sent him the two clippings. On 5 September he replied, concluding with an apologetic "Sorry, Helen, for this feeble letter – it is only the third I have written this summer." The interview with Hustak had been hurried, and he had suffered several episodes of "brain block" during it. When Hustak phoned to read the text of the article to him, he was distracted and getting ready to go to Vermont: "Instead of suggesting some changes and omissions, I blocked, panicked and said OK ... the result when it came out was for me a 'C.' Anyhow in the following Sunday's paper was the article by Ruth Wisse of McGill's Law Faculty – known by several of my contacts as a nice person but with a closed mind about certain topics. Her family perished in Auschwitz, and absolutely nothing good came out of Marx or his followers. Wisse is better at literature than at history. My impulse is to write a short letter, but it might take forever to compose."[34]

Chapter Ten

Macleod and Helen

MACLEOD MET HELEN MUSSALLEM shortly after his arrival in Ottawa in 1962. They were both active in national medical bodies, he with the ACMC and she with the Canadian Nurses Association. Macleod first refers to her in his diary on 19 February 1965: "*Te deum* – MacFarlane Report emerges from Queen's Printer. Jubilant lunch with Bernard Blishen and Helen Mussallem."[1]

Born in British Columbia, Helen was the daughter of Christian Lebanese immigrants. Her father was a fiercely independent man who moved from Eastern Canada to Winnipeg and then to the West Coast in an effort to establish himself as an entrepreneur. He learned garage mechanics and eventually established his own business. Determined that his children would become Canadians, he insisted that they speak English and forbade the use of Arabic in the home. Helen and her siblings attended public school, blending in with the other students and never experiencing any discrimination. Her father became reeve of the small suburb of Maple Ridge where they lived and was eventually elected to the provincial legislature.

After graduating from high school, Helen trained as a nurse at the Vancouver General Hospital, where she joined the staff as an operating room nurse and instructor. With the advent of World War II, she volunteered for overseas duty and worked in England and Northern Europe.

Towards the end of the war, in anticipation of the Pacific campaign, she was transferred back to Canada. Shortly after her return the United States exploded a nuclear bomb on Hiroshima, and the war ended. Using her veteran's benefits, she took a B.A. at McGill University, then went on to Columbia University in New York, where she earned her M.A. and PH.D.

It was in 1957, during her doctoral work, that the World Health Organization invited her to conduct a survey of Canadian nursing schools. As she explained it, she was "in the right place at the right time," as a doctorate was a requirement of the job. She surveyed the twenty-five schools of nursing in Canada and was appalled at what she found: "There were sparks coming out of my pen."[2] Most of the hospital schools were providing little or no education and were using the nursing students as a form of indentured labour.

This work led to additional assignments and projects in thirty-eight countries, many of them undertaken while she was the head of the Canadian Nurses Association, 1962–1981.

By April 1966 Macleod and Helen had become close friends. "Dinner at Helen's," he wrote, "gala infusion and blending of spirits – how vital and dynamic and tender this Vancouverized Lebanese. We can work at much together."[3] As the relationship flourished, Macleod recorded its progression. On 12 March 1967: "Dinner with Helen – Blessed Night."[4] On 9 April, on his return from Edmonton: "Divine rapport."[5]

On 27 April, while he was visiting Antigua and Martinique, Helen unexpectedly appeared, "like the sunshine – gay – endowing everything with a golden glow."[6] In May he informed his son Peter and daughter-in-law Margaret that he and Helen were devoted to one another. They were thrilled. "How lucky I am," he concluded.[7]

On 24 June he wrote, "Bliss was it on that day to be alive – I am sure that our destiny lies together."[8] A few days later: "I am experiencing an extraordinary feeling of benign or benevolent detachment dependent in large measure on the fact that I'm sure of my security with Helen. I hope I can be fair to her. I admire her rare honesty and humility and her tremendous dedication to her task, which I should emulate. I love her very very deeply."[9]

In May 1968 Helen was awarded an honorary doctorate by the University of New Brunswick. Attending the festivities, Macleod observed, "She's relaxed, amused, interested, and the most popular recipient." A week later he had dinner with her, but the evening ended on a low key when she told him she doubted his sincerity.[10] She seemed to have a more realistic approach to their relationship than he did.

In July he noted, "A wonderful dinner and rapport, but am anxious and insecure in an uncontrolled and unfathomable way – the outlook marriage sometime after the ICN meeting [June 1969], and play it down for a while."[11] Helen's smoking bothered him, but she would not stop. However, at the party for his retirement from ACMC, in December 1968, he described her as "masterful and lovely."[12] By this time she had risen to the position of executive director of the Canadian Nurses Association and was sought after as a consultant, travelling widely in Europe, Asia, and the Americas.

In January 1971, when he went to Haiti, he kept her informed of his activities and frequently solicited her advice on contentious matters. In numerous letters, he attempted to foster their relationship and to persuade her to visit him: "You are right about our need to make decisions – I have to learn to be franker about things that upset me, especially in that tortured realm – the sexual. You know, I think you could bring me back to the state of earlier days, but maybe that is the oldster's clutch at older things. I know I can't expect it all, but we could talk about it. If this job looks worth doing more continuously could you negotiate a year's leave?"[13]

In a later letter, he asked, "What is your plan for the next step in setting up residence?" He offered several alternatives, including marriage, possibly in the Anglican Church in Haiti or Jamaica: "There is no doubt that absence makes the heart grow fonder. Do you think you can stand the hazards of propinquity? My periods of getting up tight may be like bouts of gout, but like gout they may submit to planned therapy. Anyhow the years are slipping by. I don't believe I would love anyone else as much as I do you (and I am not going on any searches). For my part I think we have enormous fun together."[14]

In November he was again urging her to visit. In addition to the delights he had promised in previous letters, he added "a new agenda item – to take you to a Nutrition Center and perhaps to the Albert Schweitzer Hospital, where I should make a trip anyway to discuss with Dr. Mellon some elective experience for a few students next summer vacation. Two kinds of music filter through the rain – Pentecostals singing in church on our little *ruelle* and Katherine Dunham's singers and drums at Habitation Leclerc."[15]

Helen eventually did visit him in Haiti, and they had a wonderful time, enjoying the beaches and walking in the mountains. They were equally enchanted by Haitian music and customs. But in May 1972 he confided to his diary that he didn't "feel equal to matrimony."[16] Later that month he was evaluating various briefs relating to the function of community centres, and the one from McMaster University excited him particularly; they had accomplished a great deal with a northern Ontario project and their nurse practitioner project. "This is what Helen and I should be working on together," he wrote, "if only we could work together – could we?"[17] In October he had a serious conversation with her about their future: "I cannot commit myself to a firm plan," he reported in his diary. "Why? I cannot say. Certainly there is no competition."[18]

On 19 February 1974, when his old friend Hazen Sise died unexpectedly, Macleod felt obligated to help the family. Helen resented the time he spent with them, particularly with Jola, Hazen's widow. Helen was "sad and uptight," he acknowledged in his diary, and "there will be repercussions." But "I could not do otherwise."[19]

With the progressive unfolding of his relationship with Jola, Macleod came to regard Helen in a different light. When they first met, he had fallen deeply in love with her. He remained genuinely fond of her but now wanted a platonic relationship. He wrote on 8 July 1974: "Helen – platonic level maintained, but no interest in Plato."[20] Though they saw one another intermittently, the relationship continued to deteriorate. "To HKM for dinner," he recorded on 16 October, "with real indictment and with melodramatic references to mother's death (?)"[21] On 11 February 1975, he wrote: "Helen on the phone … re 'plot to destroy her' – when reprimanded makes a 360 degree switch … the shock treatment worked and she began to talk sense. I insisted on a general friendly relationship on a platonic base."[22] However, he was upset by what he called her proprietary attitude on social occasions and found her evident efforts to restore the status quo "annoying and depressing."[23]

In March 1980 she gave Macleod a birthday dinner. It was "generous," he allowed, but "we get into the usual row." She accused him of wilful and cruel neglect on the occasion of the death of two friends. "It was very unpleasant."[24]

Despite his increasing attachment to Jola, Macleod maintained an interest in Helen's work and they consulted occasionally. In May 1980 he was awarded the Order of Canada, and at the installation in October he

Wendell with Helen Mussallem (left) and Wendy (right)
at the Order of Canada presentation, Rideau Hall,
Ottawa, 15 October 1980

was accompanied by Helen and his daughter, Wendy. The erratic relationship continued over a period of years, with Macleod recording in
March 1985, for example, that Helen "blows her fuse" when he forgot
an important dinner engagement.[25] Nevertheless, she played a central role
in organizing his eightieth birthday celebration, and in successive interviews in April 2004 and again in December she had nothing but praise
for him as a man, a colleague, an intellectual, and a friend.

At one time Macleod had wanted to marry her, but she had doubted
his intent. As events played out, she was probably right. It was Jola who
suggested that Helen was too competitive: "What he needed was a
woman to take care of him."[26]

Chapter Eleven

Macleod and Jola

———□———

IN FEBRUARY 1974 Hazen Sise died suddenly of a pulmonary embolus resulting from thrombophlebitis. He left behind his wife, Jolanta ("Jola"), and a young son, Hazen ("Hadie"). Macleod wrote that he was "shocked by the tragedy. Hazen had so much yet left to do."[1]

Jola and Macleod had met in Ottawa in 1972, and "then, of course, we went to China in 1973." Alert to the family's distress, Macleod began to spend a great deal of time with Jola. Helen Mussallem considered his attention excessive.[2]

Jola felt guilty about her attitude towards her husband's illness and death: "I had given up fighting for Hazen [and was] actually fighting with him about things, which I am certain contributed to the deterioration of his health and spirits. Partly for self-protection, and partly for Hadie's sake, I did not want to move to Ottawa, as I felt I did not have the strength to cope with everything in new surroundings. I know how much pain this caused him and how badly he was disappointed with me and this is something one cannot forgive or forget easily especially when it's no longer possible to make up for it."[3]

In an undated letter written shortly after Sise's death, Macleod wrote to Jola:

I realize how distraught and despondent you must feel again and again, and isolated, even amputated in spite of support and tender concern on the part of your closest friends. My own vulnerability (in '66, more than in '42, but perhaps I forget) extended into many months. Once, when I thought myself stable, I ran into Eugene Forsey in the bank. He said something, very little, but sympathetic, I couldn't speak or see because of that lump in my throat, and eyes full of tears. The only solace I can offer is that when time passes, eventually one becomes able to think and even to talk about that hundred and one precious vignettes of the unique companionship that seems wiped away. But it doesn't disappear – so much has been built into your own bank of memories and thought habits – and they continue to be drawn upon, with less and less pain but more and more appreciation and gratitude for that priceless life experience. Your own fine qualities of character must actually accentuate your feelings of loss and deprivation, but they will also help you to emerge from the shock state – perhaps even gain a new dimension of contentment even when tinged with sadness.[4]

Jola visited Macleod at the end of April, and they spent "a lazy and delightful day at the Arboretum," he reported, "very congenial. She will emerge, will I? (despite the gap in age, distance and friends.)"[5] He later recalled "that happy lunch ... when so much conspired to transport me into a mood I had almost forgotten ... but chiefly you ... your wonderful blend of wit, whimsy and quietness, and with spring bursting out all over a feeling of new life starting."[6] In June they met again, and Macleod wrote: "Memorable rapport, and I think this is it. Despite 22 years difference and reduced virility (mine). She is congenial, warm and quiet and has a delightful sense of the ridiculous."[7]

Jola was born in 1927 to a landed family in the west of Poland, and on the outbreak of war in 1939 was deported to central Poland with her family. There they lived with relatives amid great hardships. Her father, a Polish army officer, was arrested and tortured. Jola and her mother both worked in the Resistance. In a letter written sixty years later, she recalled her postwar experience. Terrorized by the Russians, she managed to escape to Sweden, "where I arrived hidden in a coal boat a day before Christmas 1946."[8] After living in Sweden for five years she was brought to Canada by relatives. She met Hazen, an architect working for the National Capitol Commission in Ottawa, through Polish friends.

"Wendell really helped me to cope with Hazen's death, telling me about his own experiences and feelings about the death of Margaret and Jessie. I had to cope with Hazen's death, with the care of my son, my job, and my mother's health problems in Poland. Wendell was supportive in every respect. I was full of admiration for Wendell then, as I was to the end. He was a very special person, his warmth and love of people, the breadth of his interests and his intellectual achievement, his wisdom and understanding are incomparable. There was an aura of goodness surrounding him and people reacted to it. He chose not to see evil in people or their sometimes unacceptable behaviour. He was very supportive and acted as a role model for my son. Pete and Marg [Macleod] have been very kind to me, although at first they were a bit wary as to what I was about. I suppose there were hundreds of women who were interested in Wendell."[9]

At the end of November 1976, Macleod was trying to decide whether to renew his lease in Ottawa or move to Montreal to be with Jola. He decided to remain in Ottawa. "My life is too complex at the moment," he wrote. "Jola is not ready ... still too close to Hazen ... I have been too selfish and presumptuous, but very lucky ... I am encouraged. She is intelligent, kindly and responsive to the needs of others. I believe I care for her tenderly and deeply, but am afraid of my rigidity."[10] He wanted to marry her, but Jola felt that marriage would simply create problems in what had become a caring relationship.

As she wrote to him, "What I wanted to tell you is what I hope you know, that I am terribly attached to you – on the other hand I don't seem to be able to decide whether we should be happy to eat breakfast together on a permanent basis. In fact, the way I feel right now I don't know whether I want to eat breakfast at all, even alone. You are being wonderful to me, understanding, patient and supporting, but by now I feel that I am sponging on you and not giving you anything back. At first I thought I was too shocked and unbalanced to make a decision and the slightest extra pressure was just too much to take, but by now the little wheels should start turning and I feel thoroughly guilty towards you. I am not trying to ask you to be more patient with me, maybe just trying to explain something I don't understand myself in myself. One thing I want to ask you is to please give me a kick when you feel I need it and please don't be so selfless. One thing I am almost sure of is that I feel happiest or securest lying quietly within your orbit, but that does not entail much action."[11]

A visit with Jola to St Sauveur on 27 January 1978 brought back memories for Macleod of his first visits to the Laurentians with Margaret. He recorded: "I still feel the same way about Jola, with increased feeling of a common bond being strong enough to maintain companionship but for how long? Real guilt of depriving her of other contacts, and Montreal and Ottawa have been more separate this year."[12]

Meanwhile his relationship with Helen was becoming difficult as she accused him of "wilful cruel neglect etc."[13] But Jola, too, was struggling. "Jola is blue about so many problems," Macleod wrote, vowing to be "more supportive, less selfish and more sensitive."[14]

He celebrated New Year's Eve in New York with Jola, her sister Maka, and Hadie. They attended the Metropolitan Opera for the premiere of Alban Berg's opera *Lulu* on 29 December 1980. Teresa Stratas performed in the starring role. There were visits to museums and galleries and a good time was had by all.

The relationship continued to mature throughout the first half of the 1980s. In 1985 Macleod decided to move to Montreal and live with her. As Jola remembered: "On the whole he was in excellent health, although he had an operation to remove an intestinal tumour which was non-malignant, and suffered a pulmonary embolism in 1999." Despite his failing memory, "he was never difficult to look after. It was I who was looked after by Macleod. It was a difficult time for me as I found my job increasingly difficult, combined with my frequent trips to Poland to look after my mother and the responsibility of looking after my son. It was Macleod who helped me and not vice versa."[15]

Macleod spent much of his time writing letters to friends and relatives. He made occasional trips away. In 1990 he and Jola were still living a fulfilling life together. They had many friends and interesting intellectual activities, attending lectures, movies, and concerts. Macleod remained involved with Frontier College, the Norman Bethune Society, Bethune College, and McGill University, and he made trips to Ottawa, Toronto, and New York. He liked going for long walks on Mount Royal. He attended church regularly and was helpful in the garden, raking leaves, weeding, and shovelling snow. Jola only began to notice signs of significant dementia in 1995: "He was sometimes vague, or distraught or forgetful, but so is everybody else at that age. I never found him difficult to manage and one could almost always reason with him. He was always very patient with me when I got angry with him for doing something dangerous, but I don't think he realized what I was angry about."[16]

Wendell, cousin
Nancy Vining, and
Jola, celebrating
Wendell's ninety-
third birthday,
Villefranche,
March 1998

In June 1993 Macleod wrote: "A critical realization of my increasing incompetence (e.g., paying bills twice, forgetting basic things, desk
is a mess, but that is not new), but I don't know how I can improve.
Shifting papers is an old addiction! A feeling that I am in the early stages
of 'mind loss.' Therefore lifestyle changes are essential: – tidy up desk,
pay bills – reduce mail drastically – ask Jola to be accountant and book-
keeper – sort out apparel in front room closet – re-examine BC trip in
Sept. – check on details of will."[17]

In 1994 he and Jola began spending their winters at Villefranche on
the French Riviera, a place suggested to them by Macleod's brother
Archie. The trips were a great success, and they returned for several
years. They rented a small apartment with a view of the bay and the old
city of Villefranche. They had friends staying at the same place, and
Macleod celebrated his ninetieth birthday there. He attracted people

wherever he was. If he stood on a street corner waiting for the bus, Jola said, there would soon be three or four people around him engaged in conversation. He was interested in so many things and he enjoyed drawing people out. In France, well into his nineties, he still enjoyed conversing in his execrable French.

In a letter dated July 1996, he wrote from Montreal: "Jola has written well, but I, with two hands, have much trouble – on two major accounts; this two-handed script is hellishly slow and I forget often to whom I am writing. However, I improve as I contemplate our escape on Feb. 2 *au sud de France* – at least it has been semi-miraculous for four or five trials in the past. We stay in a pleasant spot, Villefranche, east of Nice on the way to the Italian frontier, which I recommend warmly."[18]

But as Macleod's dementia worsened, Jola found the strain taking its toll. Eventually she asked his son and daughter-in-law to look for a place for him for the future. Peter and Margaret decided against a veterans home in Montreal in favour of the Rideau Perley Veterans' Home in Ottawa. Jola says she "gave Peter and Marg a very hard time," as she questioned the decision to put him there. "This was the only time that I regretted not having married Wendell, as I would have had more legal rights to counter that decision."[19]

Macleod died in the spring of 2001 while he was with Jola at her summer place on Lake Champlain, his curiosity and wonder at the ways of the world unabated. His last words, fittingly, were: "What's happening?"

Wendell at age 94 at Jola's summer retreat, North Hero, Vermont, 1999

Afterword

Macleod the Man

EVEN A CURSORY READING of the preceding pages on the professional life of Wendell Macleod confirms the infinite variety of experiences that made up that life. The brief essay that follows tries to convey
some sense of the man himself – the person perceived not only by his
friends but also his detractors. To everyone, friend or enemy, he was a
dynamic presence. For every unwavering disciple, an equally fervent opponent denounced his social agenda as dangerous, even radical. But
such attacks only strengthened his faith in his own beliefs and his determination to defend them.

At its core Macleod's philosophy was founded on the basic precepts
of Christianity. He observed his religion in a way that his Presbyterian
forbears would have approved. His religious convictions were a private
matter, not something to be displayed in the public square. He chose to
live his life as a pragmatic application of Christ's teachings; he believed
that social change was possible, and to that end he devoted his life. His
message was one of hope, strengthened by his belief that social inequities
could be remedied. Perhaps because medicine was his chosen profession, he recognized the discrepancies in the quality of health care for
different groups, and strove throughout his long life to remedy the situation. In his own words, "I saw that the poor were sick in different
ways than the rich."

He came to realize that the key to any truly effective reform in medical practice must begin with a radical reform of medical education.

Crucial to this reform came the emphasis on each patient as an individual, with a unique history and experience. Vital to this approach was the nurturing of curiosity in each student, not limited to medical education. He believed that the best teachers, and the best teaching methods, imbued students with curiosity – a need to dig deeper, to question, and to reach beyond the given wisdom of the day. This emphasis on the value of curiosity as a vital component of any educational experience can be read as another expression of hope, one more facet of his religious principles in practice.

During his term as executive director of the ACMC he put into practice his basic beliefs about medical education. He literally created the ACMC as a functional organization and set up its research arm, which yielded valuable information on the demographics of Canadian medical education. He also became heavily involved with the Milbank Foundation Scholars Program of identifying and assisting the development of promising young medical educators in Central and South America; he considered it one of his major contributions to medical education. He was responsible for organizing a number of important international meetings that advanced new ideas about medical education in the Americas. He never really received due recognition for these contributions. Although he was not always successful in his efforts, as in the Haiti experience where he was hamstrung by an autocratic regime, he never gave up trying.

All this said, he was no plaster saint. He loved social gatherings – the conversation, the laughter, the good times. He loved the theatre and music, read widely, and travelled the world. He was a charming man, elegant in appearance and deportment and possessed of a wonderfully dry wit, which he used to advantage. In all, he possessed a quality best described as charisma. At any social gathering he somehow enhanced the occasion. Whether or not this quality was an expression of his religious faith is unknowable.

The story of Macleod's life emphasizes hope, a determined belief that life could be better for the world's less fortunate. Until extreme old age stopped his efforts, he pursued his Holy Grail, sometimes successfully, sometimes not. It is fair to say that he viewed his life from beginning to end as a work in progress.

His peripatetic childhood as a son of the manse in a series of communities throughout eastern Ontario and Quebec may well explain his peripatetic career. His adult life followed the same pattern of frequent relocations and professional positions. With each new phase of his life, a new challenge beckoned, reviving his fervour – his hope. Though the reality might fall short of the expectation, his initial fervour carried the day, nowhere more effectively than in his stint as dean of medicine at the University of Saskatchewan.

One of his reasons for accepting the position in Saskatchewan was his realization that, for him at least, the day-to-day practice of his profession was not enough. His nature demanded more, and the Saskatchewan offer promised to fill that void. His decision was informed by his capacity for hope for the future – his own and that of his profession. In medical education he saw his opportunity to effect change.

With something close to missionary zeal, he recruited his faculty from Canada, the United States, and Britain. During the postwar years, the idea of a full-time faculty was just beginning to gain acceptance in the United States and elsewhere; to create a new medical school in what was then (and possibly now) perceived generally as Canada's hinterland was a bold step. But at that particular juncture Saskatchewan was receptive to progressive ideas and to people like Macleod. With the CCF's election to power in 1944, the newly installed government was resolved to honour its election promise and introduce a universal health care plan in the province. A vital component of this plan was establishing a four-year, degree-granting medical college. In this endeavour Macleod was creating Canada's first postwar medical school and undertaking a new and relatively unfamiliar revision in medical education. If, in the end, to the disappointment of many of his supporters, he moved on to other challenges in other places, he must be credited with this achievement.

His admiration for Norman Bethune led eventually to Canada's recognition of the Bethune legacy. His work with the Bethune Memorial Committee, his visits to China in 1973 and 1978, and his lectures and writings awakened Canada to the momentous changes occurring in China in the areas of medical education, health care, and social reform. His role in organizing the 1979 conference on Bethune at McGill University and the subsequent publication of *Norman Bethune: His Times and His Legacy* helped to demonstrate Bethune's impact on Chinese and Canadian international and medical relations.

Macleod's work with the IDRC on the Cuban and Chinese health systems provided a critical analysis of how poor countries could use their resources to effect major public health improvements in the face of economic difficulties.

How did he do it all? Essentially, he was a consummate salesman who swept others up with him in his own passion. At least some part of his success can be traced to his student days in the late 1920s when he spent several summers as a purveyor of pots and pans. Like the more recent phenomenon of Tupperware, the merchandise was unavailable in stores. Salesmen, most of them young men, and often students, made presentations of the wares in private homes. In his late eighties Macleod could still remember the sales strategy and recite the sales pitch step by step. He believed in the quality of the merchandise, and his belief must have resonated in every word. The first day of the presentation was devoted to demonstration, but no sales were allowed; on this point he was adamant. On the second day the prospective customers were allowed to purchase to their hearts' content, and did. In the summers that he plied his craft, Macleod's sales ranked among the highest – if not the highest – in the company.

The skills he acquired in those summers served him well. As housewives had responded to the marvels of waterless cooking, so his prospective faculty reacted to his vision for the newly expanded Medical School at the University of Saskatchewan. The added innovation – the idea of locating the medical college on the university campus adjacent to a university hospital – may well have supplied an added inducement.

In his quest he was guided by his religious beliefs, but beyond those, he found inspiration in other sources. He loved poetry and often recited his favourite passages. Among these were John Donne's sermons, most specifically the passage that begins "No man is an Island," which he copied into his journal. Alfred Lord Tennyson's "Ulysses" was another favourite, particularly the idea that "'I am a part of all that I have met." But his quest was not for the usual attributes of power and fame. Rather, he envisioned a society more aware of its less fortunate members – one that recognized social and racial discrepancies and fought to eliminate them.

For all his gentleness, he could, if pushed too far, assert himself in surprising and unconventional ways. He was a determined, stubborn man, a formidable opponent in any contest of wills. Whether he even understood this quality in himself is debatable. His wife Jessie once hurt him when she said, "Whatever happens, you always get what you want." In the area of social commitment and pursuit of his goals, he believed in himself implicitly. Beneath the quiet voice and amiable demeanour lay a steely core of conviction that guided and informed everything he undertook. Perhaps this explains some of the hostility that he from time to time aroused.

Others ascribed a kind of weakness and naiveté to qualities that he projected, and they acted on that interpretation. When their lack of discernment misled them, they felt a sense of betrayal and consequently anger. In his life and work he experienced more than his share of animosity, and for the most part forgave his persecutors. Yet he was no saint or martyr. He was tough, with his beliefs grounded firmly in his childhood influences and developed through interaction with many mentors.

One anecdote confirms this quality. In the period preceding the provincial government's introduction of universal health care program, Macleod attended a social gathering in Regina. In the course of the evening an argument sprang up between him and a prominent Regina physician. A challenge was issued and accepted – terminating in a wrestling match. As a former member of McGill's student wrestling team, Macleod quickly silenced his critic. Perhaps an added bonus of this encounter was that it might well have silenced other potential critics as well.

He was an outspoken advocate of comprehensive, government-sponsored medical care programs. His early experiences with the less fortunate had convinced him that only through such a system could adequate medical care be available to all. But in a less readily definable way, his vision ranged far beyond such specific measures. In the final analysis, Macleod seemed to embody a sense that things should be better, and that, with some thought and some hard work and intelligent planning, they *could* be better. How did he justify this hope, this belief? As he often observed, "After all, homo sap is not yet fully evolved."

As we noted earlier, Macleod had his critics, those who perhaps distrusted his gentle demeanor or even his charm. One such opinion, cited in an earlier chapter, has some merit. Wilder Penfield, the pioneering neurosurgeon from the Royal Vic in Montreal, expressed some doubts about Macleod's suitability for the post of dean of medicine in Saskatchewan, suggesting that he might be "perhaps too kindly disposed and too unwilling to believe in the shortcomings of others. This resulted in his urging the candidacy of certain young physicians who were accepted in the Royal Victoria Hospital, and who, perhaps, were unwisely chosen." Penfield acknowledged that the observation was not his own but came from someone else. To some degree, his informant was correct. Macleod's need to see everyone and everything in the best possible light led to some misjudgments and, therefore, to some mistakes. But for the most part his decisions were sound, and he survived his occasional errors.

At the time of his death an obituary appeared in the *Green and White*, a University of Saskatchewan campus publication. To anyone who had known Macleod, the account of his life and his accomplishments was perfunctory. Dr T. McLeod, dean of commerce during Macleod's term as dean of medicine, wrote to protest the entire tone of the piece. He defended his former colleague vigorously and in that defence provides a vivid picture of Wendell Macleod in his prime, energetic, dedicated, competent and inspiring:

I have just worked my way through the recent edition of the Green and White. The obituary on page 29, "Recognizing a Legacy," written in memory of the first Dean of Saskatchewan's College of Medicine offering the full M.D. degree, provokes this response. The Dean's photo identifies him as John MacLeod, a first name which few outside of the family might recognize. He was generally known formally as J. Wendell Macleod, and John might indeed have been his first name, but within the circle of his friends and associates, which was a remarkably large one, he was known only as Wendell.

Those of us that were privileged to work with Wendell (I was as a member of the University Hospital Board and chairman of its Finance Committee throughout the early years of the new College of Medicine) could only marvel at his dedication to the job he had undertaken and the skill with which he literally created a new institution. Within a short period of time he drew around him a remarkably competent, even outstanding group of associates who, together, made sure that that body was founded on solid rock. Once I asked a member of the new faculty what had brought him to Saskatoon. His comment: "Wendell was a Pied Piper."

The contribution he made to the University of Saskatchewan was a great and a lasting one and is to be recognized as such. I fear that the off-hand designation set out in the Green and White reflects more a pro forma bow to the necessity of the occasion than an attempt to get at what an outstanding dean and Professor accomplished in his time on the campus.

> T.H. McLeod, One-time Dean of Commerce,
> U of S, One-time Dean of Arts and Science and
> Vice Principal, Regina Campus.

The "pied piper" analogy is apt. In the German tale, the piper is described as "pied" – "variegated" and "luminous" – because of his multicoloured clothing, presumably an attraction to the children he spirits away. In this phrase we come close to the sense of excitement and anticipation that, at his best, Macleod inspired.

After speaking with him in 1992, Anne McDonald wrote, "He sought a New Jerusalem, an Edenic world where everyone behaves with decency and common sense." As the Dutch scholar Erasmus said of his friend Sir Thomas More, Wendell Macleod was indeed "a man for all seasons." In old age as in youth, his curiosity remained unquenchable.

Appendices

Early Publications of J. Wendell Macleod Relating to a Curriculum for the New College of Medicine: A Summary

———□———

"How Healthy Is Canada?," Fourth Annual National Conference of Canadian Association of Medical Students and Interns (CAMSI), McGill University, March 1941

Macleod's topic as part of a symposium at the CAMSI conference was "the inadequacy of medical care in Canada – the general problem." At that time stationed in Halifax, where he was a Surgeon Lt. Commander in the RCNVR, he was intimately acquainted with the crowded and poor living conditions of the naval personnel. This seminal paper predicted the direction he would take in the years to come. He was, as always, ahead of his time.

He wasted no time in coming to grips with the question – which he identified as "the changing concept of health responsibility." He asked, "Is the health of the individual his own private problem, or does it concern society as a whole?" He argued that this had been the case, but changes in society (industrialization, division of labour, and the push for increased productivity) had led to the gradual shift towards the view that the health of each citizen is a matter of practical importance to the welfare of the nation as a whole.

Macleod believed that just as we now grant a certain standard of education as the birthright of every Canadian, so were we also coming to believe that every Canadian had a right to a healthy environment characterized by good public-health services organized on a community basis. He contended that by contrast health care was abysmal and poorly organized. He based his conclusions on the recently concluded "Study and Distribution of Medical Care and Public Health Services in Canada 1939." The national data showed that in every aspect of health statistics, Canada lagged far behind other countries and experienced a wide gradient of rates (deaths, infant mortality, deaths from preventable causes, deaths from tuberculosis) from province to province, with the highest rates in the poorest provinces and cities. Low-income people experienced sickness more frequently, their illnesses lasted longer, and their mortality was greater.

What should be done? Macleod's immediate answer was "spend more money, increase public health personnel, extend our facilities, provide good hospitals, train more doctors and nurses and make the facilities and services readily available." He contended that the obvious way of accomplishing this was to invoke the insurance principle of spreading the costs of illness over time and large groups. He pointed out that this was already happening and that Associated Medical Services was offering full medical care insurance for $2 a month, but even that was too much for many workers. He concluded, "To many of us now it seems only an academic exercise to debate whether health insurance should be voluntary or compulsory. We can read history; we can see the writing on the wall; we know what has happened in the last 50 years in Britain, Scandinavia, Germany and France, and we can see the trend right here in Canada. Why should we not take advantage of the experience of others? Why make costly mistakes that are not necessary? Why not give our people the benefits of still another kind of social security in our time? Whatever system we devise for the spreading of the costs of medical care we must make sure that it does not cramp us in our efforts to provide the best type of care, the one which in the light of the science of the day will most effectively prevent disease and cure it."

He then addressed the interns and medical residents: "You will be told that you are wrong, that you are pursuing blind alleys, that it was never done this way before. Turn a deaf ear – your inspiration and encouragement will come from those masses of people, young and old, who wish to receive your medical attention without suffering hardship or loss of dignity."

"Medicine Comes of Age," University of Manitoba Medical Journal
(19 November 1947)

In this seminal article, Macleod stressed the evolution of medicine as a social science. He quoted R.B. Allen of the Commonwealth Fund: "Medicine is coming of age as a social science in the service of society. It takes a man, not a machine to understand mankind."

Allen's statement, he wrote, "epitomizes present day trends which are of the greatest importance to medical practitioners of the future. Not only have they an academic bearing on the relation of medicine to other branches of learning, but they concern also the very art and technique of handling patients."

In this article Macleod stressed two important points that greatly influenced the evolution of medicine: the growth of knowledge in the physical sciences and the fragmentation of medical knowledge. He wrote: "In each historical era, medical theory and practice have always mirrored closely the philosophy and dominant interests of the times. It was inevitable, therefore, that the efflorescence of physical science during the past century should have produced an intensive application of scientific curiosity and method to such aspects of disease as could be studied under the microscope and in the test tube. The result has been an accumulation of knowledge of biological phenomena unparalleled in history, and ... methods of disease control which have helped determine the course of history ... Coincident with this amalgamation, however, there has been a fragmentation of medical knowledge and practice into a variety of clinical specialties, an inevitable result of the growth of medical science."

Macleod pointed out that the intensive study of particular anatomical structures and their function led to the development of complicated diagnostic and therapeutic techniques, some of which require so much time and special skill that they have become the property of specialists. While the process had enriched our understanding of disease and led to improvements in treatment, it had also led to our "knowing more and more about less and less" and tended to focus the attention of both doctor and patient on a particular organ or system, overlooking the relation of the organ to the body as a whole, or the significance of the symptoms to the patient as a living human being.

Macleod believed the problem had its roots in the failure to train physicians to practise what his mentor, David Barr of Cornell University, called "comprehensive medicine" or "holistic medicine." In its modern setting, it called for a judicious exploitation of all that laboratory science had to offer in the elucidation of the secrets of health, and also demanded a knowledge of human behaviour – the physiology and pathology of human personality, individually and in groups.

Thus the scope of medicine extended far beyond the study of the minutiae of disease and included a study of the socioeconomic factors that frustrate our best therapeutic efforts: "Our responsibilities are extending beyond the formalities of therapeutics, and concern society's efforts to organize for its own welfare. For the doctor, this carries new duties of citizenship as one of the implications of medicine coming of age as a social science in the service of society."

Appointed dean of medicine in 1952, Macleod spent the first year of his tenure travelling widely in Europe and the United States, visiting medical schools and consulting with experts in medical education and health care. He returned frequently to Saskatchewan to report on his travels and to provide input to local physicians and teachers about the nature of the medical college he was preparing to lead. His ideas and plans were incorporated into several papers published in the *Saskatchewan Medical Quarterly* in 1952 and 1953.

"The New School," SMQ *16 (5 September 1952)*

Macleod identified the planners of the "new school" as a large and disparate group of individuals and organizations: university staff members of the existing two-year school, and members of the advisory committee of the College of Medicine, a statutory body constituted by the University Act and analogous to councils advising other colleges made up of the president of the university, the dean of medicine, a representative of the College of Physicians and Surgeons of Saskatchewan, two government representatives (deputy minister of health and one other government representative), and representatives of urban and rural municipalities. The planners were supported by the generous interest of the Commonwealth Fund and the Rockefeller Foundation.

Macleod summarized the goals of the new school as follows:

1. The provision of a sound basis for the doctors, nurses, and other medical personnel required for that part of the Canadian middle West.

2. The arranging of suitable continuing education throughout the professional lifetime of each member of these groups.

3. The constant evaluation of the health needs of the people of the province and the gearing of undergraduate and postgraduate teaching to promote provision of the best possible medical care.

4. The conduct of appropriate research in the basic medical sciences, in the clinical academic fields and in those aspects of the social sciences pertaining to medical care.

"Were the sole purpose of extension of our present two year school the production of more Saskatchewan doctors," he wrote, "it would be much less expensive for the government to subsidize other medical schools to receive our students for the completion of the course. No, the present project is justified because it is believed that a complete medical school in the most progressive sense will contribute greatly to the health and welfare of the people of this province."

Macleod also asked what kind of doctor they wished to produce: "There appears to be agreement that what medical education needs most to do is to devise the training of a family doctor who will best meet today's needs. The mechanization of so much of medicine, the dividing up of so many skills into specialties, the persisting belief by both public and doctor that many should master most of these skills – these are but a few of the vexing questions of our medical generation. Much of medical care should return to a family unit basis. Only after deciding the kind of doctor we wish to develop, and the kind of job he is to do, can we discuss profitably the kind of teachers and the kind of curriculum that will be required."

"Medical Education in Non-University Hospitals," SMQ
(November 1952)

This paper referred to the visit to Saskatoon by John Leonard, education director of the Hartford Hospital in Connecticut, which had developed an outstanding program of intern training and practitioner involvement in a non-university hospital. The Hartford program included intern training, a quality education program, a tradition of consultation, regular rounds, and a sharing of expertise – "to share in his chief's thinking and to contribute to it."

The reason for bringing Dr Leonard appears to have been Macleod's determination to promote programs of intern and practitioner training in other hospitals in the province, and to show that a non-university hospital could become an important asset in medical education in Saskatchewan. Unfortunately he did not seriously pursue this objective during his tenure, nor did his successors. As late as 1998 Dean David Popkin was proposing the "creation of a medical college without walls," in which students would receive their education, carry out research, and provide medical services, not just in Saskatoon and Regina but throughout Saskatchewan ... there would be rural and remote training sites for family practice residents and elective educational experiences for residents in the specialties in major district hospitals in rural Saskatchewan." Thus more than half a century after Macleod's proposals, some action is finally taking place to bring them into reality.

"Postgraduate Medical Planning for Saskatchewan," SMQ 17, 195 (July 1953)

In this paper Macleod recognized the growing interest in continuing medical education in Saskatchewan but felt that it must be "geared to the real issues of the day." He identified some of the problems of current efforts as failure to assess accurately educational needs and failure to use appropriate teaching techniques; too much emphasis on subject matter, rather than on the learning process in the student; and too much detail – trying to cover everything. He recommended that doctors in a community should participate in planning their own educational activity, and a major portion of it should be round-table or bedside discussion of actual problems drawn from their office or hospital experience; didactic lectures had little value. Refresher courses should be geared to the special needs of the area.

He felt there should be continuous evaluation of what was being done; for example, at the University of Manitoba, annual refresher courses were followed up by a questionnaire to the doctors who attended regarding the usefulness of the different aspects of the program. Experience from other centres such as Colorado, Kansas, and Wisconsin should be reviewed, as reported in "Some Observations on Postgraduate Medical Education," *Annals of Internal Medicine* 38, 568 (1953). Macleod advocated planning continuing medical education courses jointly with neighbouring schools in Alberta, Manitoba, Montana, and North Dakota.

He also made the following suggestions:

(1) Hospital staff activities: The educational program should not be just for interns but for the entire staff. If staff were not interested in educational activities, they had little right to have interns.

(2) Ward rounds and conferences should ensure the sharing of clinical experience, its systematic review, and the study of pressing problems with lots of involvement of the interns. They should include invitations to outside doctors to participate, with accommodations provided for them if necessary.

(3) District society meetings should include educational material.

(4) Circuit tours should be instituted, comprising a monthly or bimonthly visit to a community medical centre by a teaching team. The agenda might include a short talk on a topic of current interest, ward rounds with a conference based on cases seen, dinner, and a talk or round-table discussion.

Educationally this was sound, Macleod felt, because it dealt with actual problems on their own scene. It brought physicians, specialists, and medical scientists together on one plane. The artificial distinction between teacher and pupil was broken down, and all involved broadened their own experience and sharpened their judgment in the process.

"Medical Preceptorships in Saskatchewan," SMQ 17, 195 (December 1953)

In a paper which formed the basis of a talk Macleod gave at the annual meeting of the College of Physicians and Surgeons of Saskatchewan at Waskesiu, 27 August 1953, he considered the preceptorship as perhaps the single most important learning experience that medical students might encounter in medical school. He also considered it important because it was a method by which the new medical college could become intimately linked with the profession, and it permitted reference to important trends in medical education that were important to the success of the medical school.

He defined the medical preceptorship as a means whereby a final-year medical student could spend six to ten weeks with a doctor in practice – an ancient kind of apprenticeship going back to the time of Hippocrates but abandoned in the past hundred years. "Why do we go back to an old technique?" Macleod asked. "It would be better to ask why we ever got away from it." He attributed the change to the growth of scientific medicine and technology leading to a preoccupation with the analysis of disease, and a loss of attention to the individual human beings under study, their family setting, and social background, all fundamental to the best management of the patient. Young doctors reared in an atmosphere of specialized and mechanized diagnosis and treatment and then exposed on the wards to the late stages of disease and the toughest diagnostic problems were unprepared to meet the problems most commonly encountered in practice.

With the preceptorship, corrective measures had been introduced – students were now being trained to obtain a clear picture of their patients' mode of living, how their illness affected their occupation, and how family problems affected their health. There was increased involvement of social workers, home visitors, and other personnel. General practitioners now had an increased role in teaching.

The preceptorship was now in use in at least one-quarter of all medical schools in the United States and Canada in the fourth year when the student came into intimate contact with a good example of the normal private practice of medicine. The University of Wisconsin (Madison), with experience with preceptorships going back to 1925, was convinced that it was their most important single teaching instrument: "For 12 weeks, the 4th year Wisconsin student lives with a doctor and follows him around on house calls, office and hospital visits and night calls to see medicine 'in its grimmest form.' He must not be used as an intern ... he must see what medicine is really like. Bonds of real interest and respect are built up which frequently lure the student back to practice in that community after he has finished his internship. The preceptors are proud of their role. They demonstrate the implications of medical citizenship in a way that cannot be taught convincingly in the classroom. The medical school in turn gets feedback on how its teaching methods stand up in practical situations."

Macleod then described what he considered to be the professional qualifications of a good preceptor: "He should be wise and thoughtful – honest in recognizing his own limitations – have an open mind and a desire to improve his knowledge and performance. While the rural setting is best, it can also be successful in some larger towns and cities. Saskatchewan is a 'natural' for this kind of teaching. Our students who will graduate in 1957 (the first class to complete all of their training at the U of S College of Medicine) will have had 6–10 weeks of this kind of experience."

"Integration of Essential Portions of Specialties in the Major Areas of Medicine," CMAJ *82, (May 1960): 1126*

Presented at the Second World Conference on Medical Education, Chicago, 29 August 1959, this paper asks: "What is the proper contribution of the medical specialties to the achievement of the broad objectives of undergraduate preparation of the basic doctor?" The answer, Macleod thought, lay in consideration of trends in medical practice at the time: (a) the overly technical approach to the problems of the sick patient, mandated by an increased technical knowledge and capability; (b) a preoccupation with the financial aspects of medicine or "dollar success" as manifested by fee for service and prepayment schemes with their emphasis on the dollar value of services rendered; and (c) the high cost of medical education, favouring students from commercially oriented backgrounds.

Macleod felt that the good specialist must be both a craftsman and a perfectionist: "As a teacher it is hard for him to avoid emphasizing his special instruments and techniques and an encyclopedic coverage of his subject matter ... to reduce his lecture hours in the face of steadily expanding subject matter may produce pain and loss!" He speculated on what stimulated medical graduates to pursue various kinds of professional work: "It is likely that most specialties attract a certain number of basically insecure individuals who cannot face the rough and tumble of wider fields. Their own limitations may prevent them coping with the emotional problems of their patients."

Macleod's main point, however, was that "the specialties cannot be integrated in the major fields of medical teaching until the specialist himself is integrated in the heart of faculty activity; and the faculty cannot determine the essential portions of a specialty's subject matter, or even the full role of the specialist teacher, until the faculty as a whole engages in the most radical kind of study of its own role. This is to ponder on the role of the medical school in its university setting and in the larger community ... the specialist must become part of a team which has clear educational objectives." He felt that the presence of a strong department of social and preventive medicine would help to preserve balance and direction in establishing the proper role of the specialist in undergraduate medical education.

"Medical Education Today," CMAJ 73 (1955): 107–11

Macleod intended this article as an outline for the practising teacher or doctor of certain trends in thinking and practice "on both sides of the Atlantic."

He noted that medical education appeared to have been most robust when it reacted appropriately and successfully to three conditions: the general level of contemporary science and scholarship; the current concepts of disease and medical practice routines; and the social, economic and political climate of the times.

He spelled out the objectives of medical education as the training of doctors, nurses and other health personnel at the undergraduate level; the provision of suitable continuation studies for all members of the health team; the evaluation of community health needs, in order to define the targets of the first two objectives; and involvement in scientific research.

Given the wide scope of the objectives, it was apparent that no single curriculum could fit all the needs. Therefore the undergraduate curriculum should aim at a basic medical education, so that the graduate would emerge with (a) the mastery of certain fundamental knowledge and skills; (b) the development of a number of basic attitudes such as intellectual curiosity and integrity and the ability to face new problems critically and without prejudice, an interest in people and sympathy and responsiveness to those in need; and (c) the capacity for continuing self-education. Macleod added: "It has become trite to say that if good students are exposed to good teachers as they investigate nature and look after the sick, then good doctors will be forthcoming despite a mediocre curriculum. No matter how ingenious and comprehensive an educational program may be, it can succeed only in the limits imposed by the capacity and vision of both teacher and student."

In an era of preoccupation with the disease process, overlooking the human hosts, their families, and society, medical education had adopted a "corpse-centred" curriculum rather than one concerned with the health and happiness of living human beings. The problem was how to return medicine to its traditional link with the humanities and social sciences. Efforts to do this had included (a) restoring the personal touch; letting students educate one another; there is an advantage in having students who have had a wide variety of experiences in different fields share with one another, rather than having them all come through the same channel; (b) making the pre-med course more flexible by allowing the student to pursue an interest in depth; and (c) providing orientation courses that presented a broad-based picture of modern medicine, its origins in folklore, in the welfare movement and in scientific discovery. First year medical students were avidly interested in the moral and ethical problems of practice and their relations to religion and philosophy.

Important changes were occurring in psychiatry and preventive medicine. Psychiatry was now using its larger place in the timetable to teach the student to observe people and understand behaviour. Interviewing patients created rapport and promoted skills in diagnosis and management of anxiety states. Similarly, the new departments of social and preventive medicine had enlarged their scope and induced medical education to produce doctors with zeal for more than curative tasks, and to concentrate on the prevention of disease.

Integrated teaching was a way to cope with the ever-more-crowded curriculum that had grown to the point of almost complete inelasticity. Departmental walls had become so high that communication between teachers in different disciplines had almost disappeared. The medical sciences had grown so rapidly and broadly that much of their factual material had to be left out. Macleod suggested keeping what was educationally profitable, dynamic, or intellectually stimulating and what appeared useful in the present and foreseeable future, and establishing a committee of representative teachers to decide what to keep and what to shed.

Students must take responsibility for their own training; their identification with the teacher group and the institution in which they worked created a vital force. A team spirit developed in the apprentice relationship when teacher and student worked together on tough clinical problems, as occured in a preceptorship. In conclusion, Macleod paid tribute to the "notable experiment in curriculum at Western Reserve University School of Medicine in Cleveland." Both he and Griff McKerracher, who became first professor of psychiatry at the University of Saskatchewan College of Medicine, visited there and were greatly impressed. Macleod wrote: "The student is exposed simultaneously to an integrated approach to medical science and to problems in human relations. Probably no curriculum was ever arranged with so much premeditated planning, a fact which in itself makes for success. This is how a preceptor of a freshman group returning two years later compares his students with those of the third year of the old curriculum. They had a

Plans for a Medical College and a Progress Report, 1952-60

———◻———

Memorandum to the President for Members of the Board of Governors, University of Saskatchewan, re: Discussion of the College of Medicine, 24 June 1952, by J.W. Macleod

I General Goal

There appears to be agreement that the purpose of establishing the full course in medicine in this university is not merely the production of more doctors. Were this the only goal, it would be cheaper to subsidize neighbouring medical schools, as several states do, in the case of the University of Colorado School of Medicine, for example. Such an arrangement would provide opportunities for young Saskatchewan people to secure professional training, but it would not ensure their returning to or remaining in their native province. While the *primary* purpose of a modern provincial medical school is to produce trained personnel, a *second* responsibility is to continue education of doctors, nurses and members of ancillary services. A *third* purpose is a study of the health needs of the people of its constituency, viz., the province of Saskatchewan; *fourth*, constant evaluation of the manner in which these needs are being met, and appropriate modification of the educational machinery as called for by this evaluation. These responsibilities are shared in varying degree with the various professional bodies and with government. All must collaborate in solving the basic problems of medical care and health promotion. The *fifth* function of medical school is to engage in scientific research. Most universities consider research to be an obligation, but in some departments it is a side activity, or is even regarded as a luxury. There is an increasing conviction that medical education must be associated with research. Perhaps more than ever before the doctor and the teacher in the second half of this century must strive to possess an open mind, the constant curiosity and the discipline in observation and reasoning that are fostered so well, although not exclusively, in an atmosphere of responsible scientific enquiry.

II Trends in Medical Education
1. We are in transition from an era of preoccupation with technical methods of study of disease, specialization of skills and the division of the patient into organs and systems. There is a widespread move to return to the consideration of the patient as a whole person, each with his own family and community setting, whose health is influenced not only by bacteria, tumours, etc., but also by psychological, social and economic factors.

2. In the curriculum, this calls for more effective teaching in Psychiatry and in Preventive and Social Medicine, as well as a broader approach in the standard clinical subjects. The student should see examples of illness and its widespread effects early in his course. Later, he should have intimate contact with a good physician in his daily work.

3. The trend is to utilize the four year medical undergraduate period to inculcate general principles, leaving chiefly to the intern period the mastery of technical skills. The internship should be the point of divergence in training of the family physician and the specialist practitioner. It is in the training of family physicians that medical education has failed most seriously. The community requires (a) family physicians who are interested and skilled in health promotion and disease prevention, as well as in the management of illness; and (b) specialist practitioners who understand the relation of their specialty to the whole person and who have broad human sympathy.

4. In the most progressive schools one sees a tendency to decrease the number of formal lectures and to increase the personal contact between teacher and student in the laboratory, at the bedside, and in the consultation room. This requires more staff but promotes better education.

5. In an effort to reduce the barriers between subjects and to make the student's knowledge more useful to him, various types of "integra-

tion of the curriculum" have appeared as experiments. They depend chiefly upon the collaboration of teachers from two or more departments at symposia, round table conferences and ward rounds. Some of these are highly successful and are bound to be adopted widely. They also call for a larger number of teachers than do older methods.

III Methods – Specific Proposals for the University of Saskatchewan
1. The development of a substantial department of Social and Preventive Medicine. (a) In collaboration with the departments of Medicine, Paediatrics, Psychiatry, etc., it should endeavour to arrange a demonstration medical practice in or near Saskatoon which will subserve both teaching and research. (b) In addition to the usual Public Health lecturers it should include personnel with scholarship in related social sciences and statistical methods to study the bearing on health of Saskatchewan's environmental factors, and to use the vast data accumulating in the records of the Saskatchewan Health Services Plan for research on various morbidity problems.

2. The provision for a fourth year rural preceptorship, whereby a student would observe a good practitioner at work for two or three months.

3. The setting up of a two-year internship specifically to train graduates for family practice. This might include a locum tenens opportunity to relieve a doctor who requires vacation or postgraduate work.

4. The inviting of general practitioners in Saskatoon to rotate in admitting selected patients to University Hospital. This would benefit students and interns, teaching staff and practitioners alike.

5. The integration of intern training and postgraduate instruction on a province-wide basis through collaboration with the College of Physicians and Surgeons of Saskatchewan and the medical boards of the hospitals concerned. This has already begun in the case of the Regina General Hospital. The purpose is three fold – (a) to provide a fair distribution of intern service, (b) to improve the facilities for intern instruction and postgraduate courses for practitioners. (c) to foster the concept of regionalization – a functional distribution of health facilities (education for doctors, nurses, etc., hospital facilities, consultation services, public education, etc. around a coordinated system of major and secondary centres. In much of this the medical school's role is inevitably to stimulate, coordinate and assist rather than to direct or dictate. However, since it has neither vested interest in medical practice nor concern

for votes, there may be situations in which leadership from the senior staff of the medical school may be more appropriate than from other professional or governmental groups.

IV Clinical Staff

1. An accepted premise is that the heads of clinical departments in the University shall also be in charge of corresponding departments in the University Hospital, and these shall be "full time" appointments. By this is meant an arrangement whereby the professor, say of surgery, is centred in the University Hospital, maintains no office downtown and restricts his practice according to some arrangement. The open issues are: (1) How is the full time teacher's practice to be restricted? (2) How is he to be remunerated? (3) How large a clinical staff, full time and part time will be required? Special features in the Saskatchewan situation, which distinguish it from most other medical schools are, the small population in Saskatoon itself and the absence in the province as a whole of any appreciable number of medically indigent people. The latter have provided in most schools, the bulk of teaching material. However the growth of prepayment medical care plans and the current prosperity have so reduced the numbers of medically indigent that many schools have had to work out techniques for student and intern training in relation to semi-private and private patients. On the whole, this has had more advantages than disadvantages. There are still problems in providing adequate experience in Obstetrics, and in certain types of Surgery, but the advantages of teaching medical practice by apprenticeship in the presence of a good doctor-patient relationship are apparent if one recognizes the goals and trends described in Sections I and II.

2. The professors then must be able to receive and treat patients referred by practitioners. Generally the patients should be referred back to their doctors. By mutual consent, it may be desirable for certain teachers to accumulate considerable practice in connection with a particular line of research, e.g., congenital heart disease. However, this should be carefully regulated, and, in general, everything possible should be done to maintain and even to improve the relation of the patient to his own doctor.

3. How is the volume of such consultations to be regulated? There have been striking instances of professors engaging in uncontrolled practice to the extent of impairing teaching and research, as well as

jeopardizing relations with the practising profession. One may restrict practice by the arbitrary limitation of (a) the proportion of time spent on consultation work, or (b) the number of patients seen according to the financial yield from consultation fees ("ceiling on earnings"). This brings up the whole matter of remuneration of clinical teachers (see section V), but in any case, an atmosphere must be created in the school which preserves the values essential to its main goals, and there must be some means whereby corrective measures may be introduced if any activity becomes disproportionate, whether practice, research or teaching.

4. How large a clinical staff, full-time and part-time will be required? The size and character of the various clinical departments must depend on:

(a) *The size of the student class.* There are many reasons for maintaining the present number of 32 students per class at least until every thing is running smoothly.

(b) *The method of instruction selected.* The use of the small group and the apprentice method is strongly recommended.

(c) *The demands of the postgraduate program.*

(i) It is essential that the program of refresher courses, circuit tours, small hospital tours and practitioner conferences be effective. This should be planned jointly with the College of Physicians and Surgeons of Saskatchewan, and with the Department of Public Health of the provincial government.

(ii) In estimates of the clinical teacher's postgraduate duties, his obligation to instruct interns and to direct a resident training scheme is frequently glossed over. In terms of hours, this requires at lest as much time as undergraduate instruction. At present, it is hard to gauge the magnitude of this task, because we are in the midst of a serious intern shortage, which is not likely to disappear. We may have to re-define the role of the intern in modern hospital life. Also, as mentioned in Section II, para 5, it is our desire to foster intern training in other hospitals in the city and province.

(d) *The amount of service rendered.* We are counting on an 80 per cent occupancy of the 550 beds in the University Hospital at the peak seasons normal for Canadian prairie practice. The number of ambulatory or outpatient consultations, however, is utterly unpredictable. There may be an initial spurt, partial subsidence and gradual build up of patient volume. At present a large number of Saskatchewan residents each year seek medical consultation elsewhere (Rochester, Minneapolis, Winnipeg, Edmonton, etc.). Many will continue to do so for various reasons. There is also a large "floating" group – some without doctors, others dissatisfied with the professional services available in their community, others who are merely curious. These "shop" from doctor to doctor and from clinic to clinic. Many of these three groups will undoubtedly come to the University Hospital. It is hoped that the opportunity will be seized to inculcate more healthy attitudes towards symptoms, to strengthen the relations of a patient to his own doctor, and to ascertain the needs of various communities in respect to health facilities. In any case, the attendance of such patients at a *teaching consultation unit* provides indispensable material for senior student, intern and resident instruction and for staff research.

(e) *The special interests of the departments.* If the Professor of Medicine were particularly interested in virus diseases, he might require one or two colleagues with special experience in virology techniques. One might do chiefly research, some teaching and no clinical work. Another might do research, clinical work and little teaching. If the project became important, additional staff, both professional and technical, would be required. Thus one cannot estimate the size of a department without knowing the character of its research activity and this in turn depends largely on the interest and initiative of its professor.

(f) *The academic and teaching talent in the Saskatoon medical profession.* Excellent participation can be counted on in most fields. An important limitation is time, since the good teacher and sound practitioner tends to be very busy in practice. It will be a policy of the College to make optimum use of part-time teachers from the practising profession. Several years will be required to assess fully these potentialities.

V Conclusions re: Size of Clinical Staff

It must be apparent that too many variables exist to permit prediction of the eventual size of most departmental staffs. A roster is proposed as a working basis for budget preparation. This minimum list is made up of nine Professors or Department Heads, three Associate Professors and six Assistant Professors. This is a minimum list of full time clinical staff to be on hand when the hospital opens in 1954. A larger staff would be required in 1955 when third year students for the first time remain in

Saskatoon to complete their course. These are arbitrary estimates. They do not include members of departments of Psychiatry, Radiology, Anaesthesiology, Physical Medicine and Rehabilitation. Some of these will be listed more strictly as hospital appointees, although eligible for teaching. The question of departmental status and relationships is being studied further.

VI Method of Remuneration of Clinical Teaching Staff
The following methods are in operation in various Canadian and American universities.

A. Full Salary Paid by University (e.g., Johns Hopkins)
Usually a heavily endowed school with strong interest in research, many indigent patients and less dependence on consultation fees from referred patients. This system has a tendency to separate a teacher from community problems, except as among indigent, and from problems of ordinary medical practice. Expensive.

B. University Salary plus Earnings from Consultation Fees
1. University salary small, earnings unlimited, usually with consultation office in town (e.g. as in most Canadian schools). Practice under this system tends to supplant research and often intrudes on teaching duties. It is suitable for part time teachers, e.g. clinical lecturers.
2. University Salary Comparable to That of Professors in Pre-Clinical Departments (Anatomy, etc.)
(a) plus all of earnings from consultation fees without limit. This method is widely used but has disadvantages already mentioned.
(b) plus a portion of earnings, either up to a defined "ceiling," or to a fixed percentage, or to a percentage varying inversely with the total earnings. For example, the Harvard plan generally permits a professor to earn in fees an amount equal to his University salary. In the case of a ceiling on earnings which may be retained, the excess earnings may be disposed of in various ways:
1. All may go to general university funds, or to general medical school funds. This has obvious disadvantages.
2. All may go to the professors' own department or research, additional equipment, salaries for unbudgeted assistants, etc. Many like this arrangement, particularly specialists in profitable fields. it is discouraging to teachers who see fewer patients and at lower fees, e.g. Paediatrics. Sometimes too, it has produced "empires" tending to dominate.

3. It may be divided between the department in which the fees are earned and a special fund to be used in the medical school according to need or as a reward.

There are many variations of the above arrangements. At Washington University, St. Louis, 15 per cent of all fees are diverted to support the pre-clinical departments. At the University of Kansas, 10 per cent of the fees go to the University Hospital to defray secretarial work and other expenses of consultation work. A good many university hospitals contribute substantially to the salaries of clinical teachers, even up to 80 per cent in some Harvard appointments. At Yale University, which is heavily endowed, the full time staff receive their entire income from university salaries. Their fees are turned into a clinical teaching and research fund. Since 1949, the anticipated balance of income over expenditure has been matched each year by a donation from the corporation to establish an endowment fund for the clinical departments.

Before selecting the method suitable in Saskatchewan, one should weigh the following considerations:

VII *Financial Aspect of Medical School Activities*
A. From the financial standpoint the activities of the College of Medicine can be classified as follows:

1. Undergraduate instruction. Student fees in various schools contribute from 1 per cent to over 100 per cent of the cost of medical education, depending on the fee and the method of cost accounting. It has been customary to charge up to the cost of medical undergraduate education such items as deficits on public ward beds and laboratories, postgraduate education, nurses' and technicians' instruction and extra research. This gives rise to quite fictitious figures. At Duke University, N.C., a recent analysis of the cost of undergraduate medical education proper i.e. after deducting other forms of public service, disclosed an estimate of less than $1000 per year per undergraduate medical student. On the basis of the old accounting system it varied from $1000 in 1953–54 to $3600 in 1947–48.

2. Postgraduate and extension work. For this service teachers receive little or no remuneration. Expenses are partially chargeable to those who receive instruction (except in case of interns and residents), to the pro-

fessional bodies who are interested (e.g., College of Physicians and Surgeons of Saskatchewan), and to the provincial health department. Assistance from Foundations may be enlisted for the initial organization of this program.

3. Survey and assessment activity, as referred to in Section I. To some extent this is inseparable from postgraduate and extension work. Much of it will constitute the normal research of the Department of Social and Preventive Medicine. Because of its importance to the general public health this function should be largely supported by the provincial government, possibly with the aid of federal health grants. However, since the field is new and some of the techniques experimental, and since the advice of special consultants may be desirable in the early stages, assistance from Foundations or individual benefactors may be available.

4. Research. Much of this will be covered by grants from the National Research Council, special institutions and societies (cancer, heart, etc.) foundations and individual donors. Nevertheless the use of a research grant increases overhead or necessitates other expenses – up to 10–35 per cent of the value of the grant. It is desirable that a medical school have a fluid fund available for pilot research projects – the testing out of a new idea which if it becomes more promising may be the subject of a formal application for a research grant. Provision of this kind of exploratory research is essential to the operation of both pre-clinical and clinical departments. If it cannot be derived from a special endowment fund then it would have to be a budget charge. Here again, until department heads are appointed, no estimate can be given of the amount required. It would be of the order of at least $50,000 annually for the whole school.

5. Consultations. Considerable revenue will accrue in the form of fees from patients treated in hospital or seen in the Teaching Consultation Unit. Some of these will be subscribers to prepayment medical care plans the use of which is growing. Some will have their medical fees paid by government agencies, (e.g., pensioners). Others will be charged in accordance with the fee schedule of the College of Physicians and Surgeons of Saskatchewan, subject of course to social service department scrutiny. In some University hospitals the individual teacher bills

the patient privately and is responsible for collections, all of which he keeps. More advantageous appears to be the arrangement whereby the university bills and collects from patients treated by the full time staff in the university hospital and its consultation unit. The essential legal point, it is believed, is that this is a restricted form of medical practice organized for educational purposes and not for profit. Against such income may be charged office and secretarial expense, rent and a portion of the teachers' income, with the balance devoted to various departmental or medical school activities, as discussed in Section V. In summary, the various activities of the College of Medicine will make quite different demands on the budget – medical care in hospital and consultations will more than pay their way; research definitely increases overhead expense but will largely be supported by funds from without the university; postgraduate instruction will be partially self supporting; undergraduate teaching, only partially offset by income from student fees, will be a budget charge.

B General Principles

1. The salary arrangement must permit us to attract and hold good men. Experienced clinical teachers command higher incomes in today's market than do pre-clinical science teachers and most teachers in other faculties. Yet we must consider resources available and we must strive for a harmonious relationship between medical and other university departments.

2. The arrangement must possess stability in respect to changing economic conditions and a fluctuating clinical load. This can be achieved by making the university salary the major component of income. Earnings from consultation fees may then yield some additional reward for the teacher who carries heavier clinical responsibilities. An upper limit should be set to control any tendency that might develop to neglect research or teaching.

3. Elasticity of the plan is also desirable. It is an advantage to be able to ask a teacher to reduce his consultation work for a few months or a year, to conduct special investigation or extra teaching without imposing thereby a serious income reduction. Similarly it may be desirable to utilize some of the excess earnings of a well established and flourishing department to help develop another or to support some new project for which funds cannot quickly be found.

"Some Milestones: Discussions in Medical Education," a Summary
of Macleod's Report to Faculty and to the Advisory Council to the
College of Medicine on the Growth of the College of Medicine, 1960
(University Archives)

1953–54: Premedical Studies   Teachers were divided into five study groups, of which the most active dealt with the possibilities and advantages of overlapping arts and medical studies. Macleod noted that in Canada the trend had been to liberalize the prerequisites for medicine, in line with what was occurring at Johns Hopkins, Vermont, and Stanford. This trend had gone into reverse at the University of Saskatchewan, where an elective course had been sacrificed to make more time for organic chemistry and genetics. In 1953–54, however, a desire was expressed to study problems in pedagogy with the aid of specialists in education.

1954–55: The Third-Year Curriculum   Planning the third-year curriculum occupied the efforts of the newly arrived clinical teachers. A breakthrough was the Survey of Human Diseases course that utilized an interdepartmental approach and replaced separate classes in medicine and surgery and, to some extent, pediatrics and psychiatry.

1955–56: The Preceptorship   The preceptorship, in which the medical student spent six to ten weeks with a doctor in practice, was established as an official curricular exercise preceding the fourth year. Macleod considered this one of his major contributions to the University of Saskatchewan. The roots of preceptorship went back two thousand years to Hippocrates, but the practice had been abandoned in the previous century as the growth of scientific medicine and technology led to a preoccupation with the analysis of disease and a concomitant loss of attention to the human being under study. Young doctors reared in an atmosphere of specialized and mechanized diagnosis and treatment were then exposed on the wards of a hospital to the latter stages of disease and the toughest diagnostic problems. They were unprepared to meet the problems commonly encountered in practice. The preceptorship, in contrast, demonstrated to the student the implications of medical citizenship in a way that could not convincingly be taught in the classroom.

At the University of Wisconsin, observed Macleod, "they are convinced that the preceptorship is their most important single teaching instrument." For twelve weeks the fourth-year student lived with a doctor, following him or her on house calls, at the office, the hospital, and on night calls, seeing medicine "in its grimmest form." Saskatchewan was a natural for this kind of teaching, Macleod asserted, and it was an experience the students would spread abroad.

1957–58: Pedagogy This year marked return of an expressed interest in the more basic issues of pedagogy. George Miller of the University of Buffalo visited the college in September 1957, stimulating the Committee on Studies to define the objectives of medical education. They concluded that their task was to produce at graduation not a fully made but miniature general practitioner or specialist but rather the basic but undifferentiated doctor who would need additional training to become a family doctor, medical scientist, or clinical specialist. The student should acquire not only facts and skills but basic attitudes and habits of thinking and working. Medical education should strive to enhance the curiosity, initiative, and sense of responsibility of the student and also lay the foundation for continuing self-education throughout a professional lifetime.

As an example, Macleod cited the neurological study group that enumerated the facts and skills the graduate should possess and also indicated at every level of instruction the subject matter and teaching techniques required. None of the studies, unfortunately, resulted in much reform of the first- and second-year timetables, which continued to include 1,232 hours of instruction in a term of thirty-two weeks.

1958–59: Objectives of the Curriculum Objectives were considered in relation to the demands on the time and intellectual resources of the student. Not all students learned at the same pace; pushing a slow student too fast resulted in cramming and superficial learning. On the other hand, keeping a brilliant student to the fixed pace of the class might result in even more serious damage. Would there be value, Macleod asked, in thinking of an "irreducible minimum" of facts, skills, and even attributes that could be a goal for all students? Slower students could use the extra time to consolidate the core material, while the more advanced could use the greater freedom to work in fields of special interest.

The response to this proposal, which included electives, was varied. Some of the best teachers saw no need for it; some even thought it unsound. Others indicated that they would like to pursue it experimen-tally. Macleod concluded: "Most importantly, finally, is the evidence here and there among our 200 teachers of increasing interest in our ed-ucational task."

Appendix Three

Curriculum Planning in Medical Education for the Faculty of Medicine and Pharmacy, State University of Haiti

——□——

Prepared at the Request of Dr Alix Theard, Secretary of State for Public Health and Population, by J. Wendell Macleod, Consultant in Medical Education, Pan American Health Organization, November 1971

Macleod began his report with a series of definitions: by "curriculum" he meant the sum total of educational arrangements made formally by the faculty and related authorities to achieve specified educational objectives. "Curriculum" referred mainly to an arrangement of learning experiences which, when pursued in sequence by the student, would "permit him to achieve the levels of competence specified in the educational objectives. Evaluation of the progress of the student in achieving these objectives is a measure not only of the quality of performance of the student; it reflects also the effectiveness of the professors, the validity of the objectives, and the characteristics of the curriculum. Consequently the rational evolution of the curriculum implies constant attention to its objectives, methodical evaluation of the extent to which they are being achieved, periodic examination of the curriculum and as necessary, modification of the curriculum and of the assumptions on which it is based. The educational program is conceived then in terms of a dynamic system with defined components and a built in mechanism of feedback to improve its efficacy."

Macleod then listed a number of crucial factors to be taken into consideration when a new medical faculty planned its curriculum:

1. The social purpose or function of the Faculty of Medicine in the national setting.
2. Issues of a semi political nature that require administrative decisions at a high national level (size of class; expansion envisaged; non academic criteria for admission to the course i.e., citizenship, rural – urban or social class origin; fees; bursaries for needy students.
3. Resources available – supply and quality of applicants, professors, various facilities and financial base.
4. Contemporary pressures to which the program must adapt – socio-economic forces and the advance of science, including pedagogy.
5. Establishing the educational objectives and the curriculum.
6. Evaluation of the extent to which the curriculum achieves the educational objectives.
7. Modification of the curriculum and review of the educational objectives and if necessary, re-examination of the original assumptions and policies.

He then considered the social purpose of the faculty, and selected two issues: to offer medical education and training which would produce doctors of internationally acceptable competence; and to improve conditions of health in Haiti by carefully selected roles in teaching, service and research.

Next he discussed the contemporary pressures that might affect the program:

– The public, the world over, is clamouring for better access to the fruits of scientific advance, including a more just distribution of health services among the rich and the poor and the urban and rural sectors of the entire population.
– An adequate delivery of health care can be achieved only by broad health programs in both the preventive and curative services, and then only when the work of the physician is complemented by the efforts of other professionals and auxiliaries working as a harmoniously coordinated team. In many areas, for many years to come, the only health personnel available will be nurses and/or auxiliaries.
– In the face of such forces making for social change, the medical

profession and its leaders has been inattentive or unresponsive.
  – They must learn to understand:
  – (a) the societies that support them
  – (b) the manner in which professions adapt to social change or
forfeit their privileged position in society (c) the need, more than ever
before, for the health professions to cooperate with each other, with
government and with the general public.

Medical faculties are being urged now to pay greater attention to
social issues, to give their students useful experience in community
medicine and to engage in research on how best to provide equitable
health care in the face of inadequate resources of personnel and
money.

Scientific advance – without minimizing the enormous contribution
to human welfare made by biomedical research in recent decades, it is
clear that this progress has also accentuated problems in medical care
and medical teaching. Some of the consequences of increasing specialization and increased preoccupation with research are:
  – the fragmentation of knowledge and skills, with reduced communication between specialists
  – preoccupation with those diseases which are investigated and
treated in hospitals
  – widening gaps between hospital and community; between the
physician and the general public and between the student's interest in
scientific medicine on the one hand, and his concern for human need
on the other.

Many faculties are seeking now to present the subject matter of
medicine as an integrated whole, and to relate the work of the doctor
to the problems of human beings, individually and collectively, not just
to the mechanisms of their disorders.

Macleod then turned his attention to progress in pedagogy:

Longer than in many other fields, medical education has retained its
heritage from the mediaeval university. Professors continue to preach
dogma with an authoritarian air to students who record it passively
in their notebooks, memorize it by heart and regurgitate it later at the
examination. Only recently has attention been paid to findings in the
behavioural sciences concerning what actually takes place in learning,
teaching and education.

– Students learn at different rates and the slow learner is not necessarily the least competent in the professional role.

– Faulty medical practice appears to be due as often to faulty attitudes and habits as to ignorance.

– With regard to technical skills, a student learns little from a teacher's description in a lecture.

– He learns more when he observes the professor perform in a real situation. He learns most when he performs himself.

– To spend a long time in acquiring detailed basic information before using it is a waste of time. Typically, students will have forgotten 50 per cent of the information they acquire within a year after completing a course, and 75 per cent within two years. (Tyler).

Macleod was concerned about the issue of establishing educational objectives. He emphasized the importance of describing concretely what the student should be able to do better or differently as a result of instruction. Students should be told in advance what the educational objectives of a course, lecture or exercise were, and this information should be filed in the department and available to all interested parties. He offered the following educational objectives for the course as a whole:

As he proceeds through the medical course the student will be able: (a) to demonstrate increasing familiarity with the health problems of Haiti, and (b) competence in the performance of a series of medical roles to be specified for various stages of the course, culminating in the ability at the end of Year IV to serve as a community physician in Haiti.

– to master a common core of knowledge and skills in the major fields of medicine (but not all specialties) understanding their relationships and interdependence, in both curative and preventive aspects, in order to become competent to serve as a hospital intern and, if desired, to qualify for admission to advanced training in Haiti or abroad.

– to acquire competence in using the principle and techniques of "problem solving" in his approach to his studies and to his professional tasks in all their aspects; in this way to develop flexibility, able to discard obsolete ideas and methods and to adapt easily to new approaches.

– to master the art of learning critically and independently (on his own) and to feel responsible for continuing to do so throughout his lifetime.

– to work harmoniously with others, to communicate effectively, and to become a good teacher.

Based on the general principles elaborated above, Macleod then provided his specific and detailed recommendations for each stage of the course. The real objective was to put a spotlight on the health problems of Haiti from the very beginning to the end of the course. He suggested, for example, that the very first lecture should be a "journalistic review" of infant and child mortality in Haiti, with half of the time being devoted to the presentation of a child with *kwashiorkor* who also has enteritis. Malnutrition would be related at once to problems in food habits and taboos, purchasing power, agricultural production, sanitation, and personal hygiene. This would launch a theme to continue with few interruptions until the young graduate took his turn as a community physician, leading a team of nurses, sanitarians, health educators and auxiliaries in the care of perhaps fifty thousand people.

The general curricular advice given above was supplemented with a collection of schedules and diagrams indicating in detail the expected progress of the student through each aspect of the curriculum.

Appendix Four

Republic of Cuba: Health Care and Population – A Preliminary Report to IDRC by J. Wendell Macleod: An Excerpt

Conclusions

1. The 14 year experience of the Republic of Cuba in health care, according to reports at hand, is distinctive, significant and clearly pertinent to the concerns of IDRC. It is relevant particularly to countries with large rural populations, urgent health needs and scanty resources. Scrutiny of the Cuban experience should be rewarding also to the more affluent and industrialized societies if trying seriously to improve the overall effectiveness of their health services. The Cuban accomplishment challenges certain conventional assumptions concerning the relation of health status to socio-economic development. At the same time, it should encourage or confirm confidence in a number of current trends in concept and method which appear to be gaining wider acceptance. Because of the frank and open minded attitude of the Cubans to their own problems and their apparent eagerness to share their own and others' experience, the time seems opportune to foster closer communication and to explore with them more deeply some of the critical issues in development.

2. Depressing levels of morbidity and mortality have been attacked by Cuba with spectacular success by means of energetic planning, crash programs and mass participation of the populace. On the same scale, effective programs are well on the way to eliminating the worst concomi-

tants of poverty – squalid housing, unstable family incomes, mal-distribution of arable land, illiteracy and the attitude of fatalistic pessimism concerning efforts to better the conditions of life. These reforms spring from a rural philosophy which emphasizes the goal of equality of access to social benefits as a human right and instills confidence in the ability of people to gain them by means of group action.

3. The methods used in the Cuban advance in health illustrate realistically a number of current world trends:

(a) rational regional planning and organization of services,

(b) the extended health team with wider sharing of responsibility and closer contact with the grass-roots community,

(c) crash programs in education and training to correct shortages in manpower,

(d) greater relevance of these programs to the tasks to be performed to meet the needs and expectations of all sectors of the population,

(e) extensive involvement of citizens' organizations and volunteers in the implementation of the programs,

(f) provision of feedback from the consumers of services in order to improve them; and finally

(g) the establishment of a statistical base to permit more refined estimation of needs and the evaluation of the effect of programs as they are implemented. The relevance of all these features to the modern movement in health care suggests at once the possible international usefulness of the Cuban experience as a demonstration or teaching model for study and emulation by nations with widely different needs and resources. Cuba's experience, in due course, should yield data of particular value to ministries of health, planners in cabinets and treasury departments, schools of public health and researchers in the related social science fields.

4. Already the emerging Cuban "case history" has challenged the prevalent assumption that a satisfactory health status cannot be attained in a setting where the national economic base is marginal. The evidence at hand invites a focus now on the question of which social values, structures, policies and circumstances are the indispensable ingredients of a poor country's effort that would erase the picture of disease and deprivation that seems to be the invariable accompaniment of poverty. Are there moral and strategic equivalents to a social revolution?

5. Concerning population phenomena and policies there is less information and some of the figures cited by reviewers are in conflict. Fluc-

tuation in birth and growth rates since 1959 have stimulated much demographic speculation ... much research is required to understand the relative influence on fertility of such new factors as full employment, more equitable purchasing power and distribution of basic necessities (but overall scarcity of consumer goods), greatly enlarged participation of women in the work force including posts of responsibility, provision of day care for children and the wide and ready availability of contraceptives as a human right – of both women and the family

Recommendations

1. An exploratory visit to Cuba by representatives of IDRC is under negotiation with the Embassy in Ottawa, with a stay of not less than two weeks being envisaged for November 1973. Pending other advice from authorities in Havana, I recommend a team with competence to observe in the fields of rural health care delivery, training of the extended health team for community service, integration of health care with other social services at the community level, demographic research and population policy.

The Significance of the Chinese Experience in Health Care

Excerpt of "Health Care in the People's Republic of China, A Bibliography with Abstracts" with Shahid Akhtar, IDRC, 1975

Macleod's contribution is based on a review of the literature on health care in China that he carried out at the request of IDRC, and on an eighteen-day visit to China in September 1973 with a delegation from Norman Bethune Medical Committee on the invitation of the Friendship Association Peking. It is an attempt to summarize the accomplishments of the People's Republic of China in the field of health, to speculate on the factors that contributed to the notable success of the effort, and to consider the question of how lessons learned from the Chinese experience may be applied in other settings.

What are the accomplishments of the PRC affecting health?

1. Reduction or elimination of communicable diseases as a major cause of disability or death – cholera, malaria, venereal disease, schistosomiasis and tuberculosis.

2. Virtual elimination of many natural disasters – famine, serious malnutrition and death from floods – due primarily to progress in agriculture, irrigation, flood control and also in public health and education.

3. Universal primary and extensive secondary education, rapid progress in reduction of adult illiteracy, and effective communication with virtually the whole population by press, radio or public loudspeaker. Healthful living is emphasized as one's civic responsibility.

4. Provision of an astounding system of primary health care, accessible to the total population of nearly 800 million and coordinated with a network of hospitals to provide care at secondary and tertiary levels. Associated with this has been the production of large numbers of various types of health personnel, particularly in the middle level.

5. Development of clinical and developmental research with active reporting in new medical and scientific journals; advances in medical technology and related concepts, e.g., treatment of burns, re–implantation of severed limbs, acupuncture analgesia etc.

6. Apparent reduction of population growth by what may well be the most comprehensive and effective program of family planning in the world.

7. Virtually all visitors report extraordinarily high morale among the Chinese people.

Why have the efforts in health care been so effective and apparently acceptable?

1. The objective of programs in health have been subordinate to but in harmony with basic social goals adopted by the nation as a whole, e.g., a classless society in which social benefits are available to all; each contributes toward the common good; rewards take into account the individuals contribution as well as his needs; ingenuity, self reliance and self sufficiency of the individual and the community are encouraged by incentives; progress in the rural sector must not be retarded by urban development.

2. Health programs are planned and carried out in harmony with the prevailing assumptions and expectations of the bulk of the people. In the delivery of primary health care many traditional beliefs and folkways are utilized rather than overlooked and rejected. There is respect for established cultural patterns. An integration of both traditional and western medicine is being attempted.

3. At the same time innovation and experimentation are being encouraged in all circles of society.

4. The system of health care is unusually flexible and adaptable to a variety of situations because of the Chinese blend of decentralization, local autonomy, and active popular participation at the grass roots level.

5. A major instrument in health programs has been the mass campaign involving huge numbers of people of all ages through their organizations at all levels of the country or commune. Apart from the effective obliteration of pests or completion of an immunization task in one mammoth effort, this approach gives insight into the problem at hand and is an invaluable experience in team work.

6. Waste and confusion are minimized by a search for a clear order of priority among alternatives. Choices tend to be related to basic social goals and realistically to the resources available and the perspective of the current stage of development. The focus tends to be on urgent problems about which something conceivably can be done, e.g.,

a. Provision of primary health care for the bulk of the people (80 per cent rural) by way of part time auxiliary workers recruited locally and trained in rural centres by experienced physicians deployed from urban hospitals.

b. Integration of preventive medical and public health measures with clinical activities, using generalist personnel in the main — hence the barefoot doctor is as much a teacher and sanitary worker as a practitioner of curative medicine and family planning.

What is the source of the PRC's wisdom and strength?

1. The influence of an ancient civilization with a rich store of accumulated experience and wisdom – intellectual, social and technical. A deeply rooted tradition of individual self discipline in deference to a respected group – family, clan or party.

2. China's present medico-political philosophy including special ethical principles. The regime places top priority, after defence, on providing all people with food, shelter, modest levels of education and health care, and a modest means of livelihood. For hundreds of millions of people this has meant decreasing shortages, increased purchasing power, but no inflation. Poverty and its consequences are being conquered. Everyone is exhorted to love and to care for one another, to practice a selfless devotion to one's tasks, and to subordinate all efforts to "serving the people." Whether this attitude will continue to prevail remains to be seen.

Which elements in Chinese experience are transferable to other settings?

1. In the health field, few if any of the components of the Chinese experience of the past quarter century have been unique in conception. Most of the principles have been advocated for decades by organisations and consultants working internationally on problems of health or community development, but seldom with comparable effectiveness or at such low cost. The answer seems to lie in the realm of social organization, mass motivation and morale – a combination not readily reproducible in the absence of an equivalent cluster of interacting socio-political circumstances and historical forces.

2. All would agree that the goals implicit in the Chinese accomplishments listed earlier should be primary objectives of health policy in any country seeking effective development in the face of massive needs and scanty resources. How many nations are both willing and able to mount such a multi-thrust attack?

3. Productivity is almost certainly enhanced by a suitable system of primary health care that is accessible to all workers and their families, rural as well as urban. The system's effectiveness depends on the extent to which it succeeds in modifying the hygienic or sanitary behaviour of masses of people and meets their expectations for attention to their health problems as they see them. These twin efforts in education and support usually fail unless those who work directly with the people are capable of understanding them, winning their confidence and animating them. Such a harmonious constructive two way relationship would be difficult to achieve within the social and historical context of many countries. Moreover, even when governments understand these more subtle requirements, they are often unable to recruit and support such personnel in sufficient numbers to cover the population. Too often the only people served are those living in or around the capital city and centres of major commerce. The Chinese system which goes a long way toward meeting these criteria is the outcome of a lengthy, indigenous socio-political process involving major and minor principles with a large degree of trial and error guidance in their application. How many needy societies would be willing to consider them? If adopted as policy could they be implemented and with what effect?

The accomplishments in health care described above are substantiated by Ma Haide (George Hatem), an American who spent many years as a doctor in China. In his contribution to *Norman Bethune: His Times and His Legacy*, he not only described the conditions under which Bethune lived and worked in China but also the changes which had occurred since then. Ma Haide describes how, with the formation of the PRC and under the leadership of the government and party, the medical workers and the public health personnel, together with the people, set up a health care system to serve the whole population ... the training of medical, public health and paramedical health workers was one of the early measures used to quickly build up an army of health professionals. At the end of 1978 there were 3.8 million health workers, including 1.6 million "barefoot doctors" and 700,000 midwives; 358,520 doctors graduated from medical colleges. In 1978 there were 1.856 million beds of which 700,000 were in the cities ... China is nearly self sufficient in pharmaceuticals. antibiotics, vaccines and other biological products.

A three-tiered national health system comprising National and Provincial Ministries of Health and County Medical Health Centres serves the whole country ... Medical work is based on a number of basic principles which include: – having health care serve the common people – placing high priorities on prevention – integrating modern and traditional Chinese medicine and their practitioners – combining health campaigns with other mass campaigns (e.g., agriculture, education and production).

Sanitation campaigns are an important part of preventive work. They revolve around the National Patriotic Health Movement which leads campaigns against "the four pests" – flies, mosquitoes, rats and bedbugs – and sanitation in the rural areas such as drinking water, sewage disposal, composting, latrines, animal pens and food hygiene. In recent years there has been added the care of the environment, smoke, air, waste water control as part of a national patriotic movement.

China Revisited, August–September 1978: Excerpt of Macleod's Lecture Given at the Manitoba Sciences Centre, 25 January 1979

In the early '50s the communist authorities introduced a "piece work" system to step up productivity; the harder you worked, the more you got, in keeping with Marxist dictum "from each according to his ability, to each according to his work." But within a year, so-called "contradictions" appeared. The selfish person benefited, the generous person who helped someone else or cleaned up the shop or yard got less. The sense of unity was damaged and productivity went down. Many workers complained: they wanted to work for the revolution, not for themselves. Piece work meant getting away from the spirit of Yennan and the long march. After a year piece work was discontinued. In 1958 there was the "great leap forward" – versatility and self reliance were emphasized – farmers were encouraged to make their own implements. There was tremendous elation, but this was blunted by mismanagement and a series of natural disasters in 1959–61. In 1960 the Soviet advisors departed with their blueprints and formulae and the Chinese had to use their own resources. After a short slump, spirits rose, Russian debts were paid and productivity began to rise again.

In 1962, strangely enough, piece work wages were started again, and again morale was damaged and productivity fell. Clearly there existed in the party leadership conflicting philosophies. One was called the "socialist road" where one put loyalty to the work brigade or the country ahead of personal gain; the other was the "capitalist road" (or the soviet union model) where one bribed the worker with material incentives. That group favoured crash programs for heavy industry; the other wished to balance industry and agriculture. There would always be the tendency for some persons to seek possessions, privilege and power.

The cultural revolution of 1966 was intended to emphasize Mao's social values and socialist approaches, cleansing the party of revisionist tendencies. The revisionist president Liu Shao-chi was expelled in 1968, and Liu Piao two years later. The latter had apparently encouraged the extremist wing of the cultural revolution to do ridiculous things – get rid of all examinations – push to the extreme service in the rural areas for managers, cadres and professors, indeed all intellectuals. The radical zealots and fundamentalists believed in a word for word interpretation of Mao's teaching as given in the Little Red Book. While they may have been sincere in their beliefs they were exploited by Liu Piao and others (the "Gang of Four") to discredit chairman Mao. They also used the opportunity to infiltrate all the power centres and to punish the intellectuals. The extremism of the zealots which continued until October of 1976 almost ruined higher education and scientific research and damaged the school system. It also reduced industrial output and lowered the quality of exported goods. There was widespread relief when the power of this group was checked.

Wendell Macleod through the Eyes of His Contemporaries

———□———

Excerpts from the Unpublished Diary of W.P. Thompson,
President of the University of Saskatchewan, 1949–60

In 1951 we began to plan the full medical course. That involved two kinds of work: (1) making the basic decisions about the structure and conduct of the course, and (2) appointing the faculty. For both purposes the first step was the appointment of a dean, and I can say without reservation that one of the very best things done for the University during my presidency or at any other time was the appointment of Dean Wendell Macleod. He is a man of great ability and complete integrity, personal charm, desirable social attitudes, and skill in handling men. He did an excellent job in relation to the fundamental planning decisions, and in directing the college for the first eight years. His resignation in 1960 after I retired was an irreparable loss. It was due to his support of the government's Medicare program which the university authorities of the time thought unwise because of the attitude of the medical profession.

I am very proud of our first group of senior appointees to the medical faculty. They included Hilliard, Bailey and Horlick in medicine, Nanson in surgery, Feindel in neurosurgery, Brown in obstetrics, Robertson and Wolfe in social medicine, a remarkably fine group of men. Of course the chief credit for their appointment should go to Wendell

Macleod but I at least deserve the credit for appointing him and helping and supporting him with all my ability and the influence of my office. Unfortunately Hilliard, Brown, Feindel, Robertson, Wolfe and Badgley followed the dean's example in resigning, some of them also because of the Medicare controversy.

I am strongly of the opinion that the appointment of faculty members is the most important, interesting, satisfying and rewarding of the numerous tasks a university president has to do. The appointment of even one very outstanding man may have a far-reaching effect for good on the long term future of his institution. Subsequently it is wonderful to be able to say with pride, "I appointed that man."

Tribute by ACMC *president Walter C. Mackenzie to Wendell Macleod on his retiring as the first executive secretary of the newly established Canadian Association of Medical Colleges (published in the* ACMC *newsletter, August 1970)*

Wendell graduated in medicine at McGill in 1930 at the dawn of the depression and pursued postgraduate training at the Royal Victoria Hospital (Montreal) and at Washington University in St. Louis. One cannot help but feel that some of his medical experiences during those dreadful years had a considerable effect on his future endeavors. The late Dr. Allan Bailey once said that "even thought Wendell's academic and material success was inevitable, whatever might come his way would never influence, make him renounce or forget the unfortunate of this world" ...

He developed an awareness of the important role that psychosomatic disturbances play, not only in the obviously neurotic patient but in the presentation of disease in all patients. He realized that little attention had been given to this phase of medicine in medical schools, He was an excellent clinician ... and had an extensive interest and knowledge of disease processes, had tremendous curiosity and as a result, an understanding of the personal qualities of his patients ...

When Wendell became the first full time executive secretary of the ACMC, the organization developed very rapidly and the secretariat became an integrated and central force in medical education in Canada. Wendell chose not to be a servant of the Board but a leader and driver of policy. He fostered a close relationship with the AUCC in spite of some conflicting interests and developed a good working relationship with them. In all of these accomplishments, Wendell was able to maintain a personal integrity with respect to his own views on medical education and medical care. There were occasions at ACMC when some Board members felt that Wendell neglected his national responsibilities and devoted too much time to outside duties (e.g., Milbank Foundation) and reminded him that he was "a servant of the Deans," but in retrospect he has done so much for medical education in North America and internationally that we now realize that he has reflected in the best way possible on the activities and stature of the ACMC. For those of us who have had the good fortune to know him personally, it is accepted that he is one of the best liked men we have all known. His general warmth of character and humility as a person have elicited a response of friendliness, and his own high ethical and moral standards have invariably been apparent in relation to his judgments. He is not one who feared to stand alone, if such a position appeared to him to be correct.

Citation of Wendell Macleod for the R.D. De Fries Award, presented at the Canadian Public Health Association meeting, 1984

Wendell Macleod enjoys the respect and affection of countless great and humble people of our time, including the students he taught, the patients he treated, and the many physicians, nurses, social scientists and community workers who came under his influence. It is doubtful that any living Canadian physician has a greater number of friends and colleagues in the field of health care and education around the world – and he usually remembers their names! He has received multiple honours – Order of Canada, Order of the British Empire (military division), honorary degrees from four Canadian universities and the Duncan Graham Award of the Royal College of Physicians and Surgeons for distinction in medical education. It is therefore fitting and appropriate that this man, who from his earliest professional years has been dedicated to the social and health goals of his profession, and has served the public's health so well for more than half a century should now receive the highest honor that can be conferred by the CPHA – the R.D. De Fries Award.

Appendix Eight

In Memoriam: Extracts from Eulogies by
J. Peter Macleod and Maurice McGregor

———□———

Peter Macleod

Many of those who knew or worked with Wendell Macleod have attempted to formulate a description of the particular qualities that made Wendell such an extraordinary individual. Energy, vision, charisma, warmth, empathy, high principles, great resolve – some amalgam of these noble elements is the likely answer, tempered by a boundless curiosity. This often led him to somehow winkle out of those he met a unique quality or experience, something of value to both the individual and the wider world of family and community writ large. Meeting Wendell was invariably an enriching experience all around. Wendell had a strong sense of family. When travelling he would go out of his way to look up distant cousins. He loved family get-togethers. He would have loved to be here, visiting with you to find out what you have been doing.

He taught Wendy and me to use the *Oxford Dictionary* and the *Book of Knowledge* to settle debates and to answer questions. He taught me that righteous indignation was the most crippling of emotions. He taught me that there was much more to treating the patient than making a diagnosis and prescribing treatment. In our rebellious teenage years we did our best to learn nothing from him and I still forget his lessons sometimes. He was a role model and advisor to three generations.

The one quality I value the most is his love of people as individuals.

Wendell had that rare ability to find something extraordinary and unique within every person he encountered. Wendell loved people.

Maurice McGregor

I am poorly qualified to talk to you about Wendell. I wish I had known him better. But I learned enough about him to develop a real admiration and affection for this gentle dynamo ... The final common path through which we eventually did get to know one another was Norman Bethune ... It is not hard to see why Wendell liked and admired him so much ... for Wendell and Bethune had much in common. Both were sons of the manse, and both were Scots. Bethune described his heritage in a letter written in 1935. "My father," he wrote, "was an evangelist, and I come from a race of men, violent, unstable, of passionate conviction and wrong headedness, intolerant, yet with it all a vision of truth and the drive to carry them to it." Though the Wendell I knew was stable as a rock and always had the steel of his convictions well covered by the velvet glove of his impeccable good manners, there is something in that description which we can recognize ... Wendell described Bethune as "informed, outgoing, dynamic in speech and body movements, cheerful and sometimes gay. He seemed to ... stimulate in us, quickly, a sense of person to person contact with him." I believe that in picking on these characteristics to extol, Wendell is also describing those things he admires and emulates, and so, describing himself ... Through Bethune he is introduced to a world of culture, of art, and to a dynamic group of friends whose passion is the intelligent exchange of ideas. I suspect that at this time Bethune played a major role in Wendell's life. As Wendell developed his own life and made his own major contributions to medicine and medical education, his commitment to honour Bethune became a recurring theme. His involvement with the new medical school in Saskatchewan ... was where he found complete fulfillment for his exceptional qualities of intelligence, leadership, and an incredibly persuasive charm. Walter MacKenzie wrote of him at the time that he was "a beloved teacher, a friend of students and an outstanding physician. He was one of the first to point out to many of us in this country that economic and social factors profoundly affected health." MacKenzie goes on: "His genuine warmth of character and humility as a person have elicited a response of friendliness, and his own high ethical and moral standards have invariably been apparent" in his judgments.

My last memory of Wendell is of his profound, his innate social grace which allowed him, even when his memory was seriously affected, to act impeccably as the perfect host to one of Jola's superb dinner parties. Wendell chose for Norman Bethune a quote from W.H. Auden. And once again, I believe it would be equally appropriate for Wendell Macleod: "Act from thought should quickly follow. What is thinking for?"

Appendix Nine

Publications of J. Wendell Macleod

———□———

AS SOLE AUTHOR

Macleod, J.W. "'Cascade Stomach' Associated with Impaired Oe-
sophageal Emptying in a Case of 'Nervous Indigestion.'" *CMAJ* 36
(1937): 242–4.
– "Intubation in Intestinal Obstruction." *McGill Medical Journal*
(1941).
– "The Inadequacy of Medical Care in Canada – The General Prob-
lem." How Healthy Is Canada? A Symposium. *CAMSI* 1 (1942):
46–8.
– "Trichiniasis in the Royal Canadian Navy." *Journal of Canadian
Medical Services* 2 (1945): 650–5.
– "Functional Disorders of the Digestive Tract." *Manitoba Medical
Review* 26, no. 8 (August 1946).
– "Medicine Comes of Age." *University of Manitoba Medical Journal*
19, no. 1 (November 1947).
– Inaugural Address. *University of Manitoba Medical Journal* 22, no. 1
(1950).
– "Duodenal Ulcers: Recent Trends in Diet Therapy." *Manitoba
Medical Review* 30 (March 1950): 150–2.
– "The Recognition and Management of Disordered Colon Function."
Winnipeg Clinic Quarterly (March 1951): 1–7.

– "The New School." *Saskatchewan Medical Quarterly* (September 1952): 50.
– "Medical Education in Non-University Hospitals." *Saskatchewan Medical Quarterly* (November 1952).
– "Postgraduate Planning for Saskatchewan." *Saskatchewan Medical Quarterly* 17 (July 1953): 195.
– "Medical Preceptorships in Saskatchewan." *Saskatchewan Medical Quarterly* 17 (December 1953): 274.
– "Medical Education Today." CMAJ 73 (1955): 107–11.
– "The University of Saskatchewan Medical Centre." *Saskatchewan Community* 7, no. 4 (15 January 1956).
– "Hospitals and the Changing Health Scene." *Saskatchewan Catholic Hospitals and Nursing Digest* (December 1956).
– "Retrospect in Gastroenterology." *Winnipeg Clinic Quarterly* 11 (September 1958): 1–8.
– "The Good Is Oft Interred with Their Bones." *Saskatchewan Medical Quarterly* 23 (APRIL 1959).
– "Alpha Omega Alpha: Foundations for the Future." *Pharos* (January 1959): 44–52.
– "Integration of Essential Portions of Specialties in the Major Areas of Medicine." CMAJ 82 (May 1960): 1126-7.
– "Basic Issues in Hospital and Medical Care Insurance." CMAJ 84 (June 1961): 1434.
– "Medical Student Enrollment in Canadian Universities." CMAJ 88 (April 1963): 683.
– "Curriculum in Canadian Medical Education." CMAJ 88 (April 1963): 705.
– "Medical Students in Canadian Universities, 1962–1963 and 1963–1964." CMAJ 90 (April 1964): 809.
– "Medical Education in Canada." *The Scalpel* 35 (Spring 1965): 110–14.
– "Education for the Health Professions to Meet Tomorrow's Needs." *Applied Therapeutics* 8 (1966): 354.
– "Education and Social Protest." *Canadian Doctor* (August 1969).
– "Medicine's Responsibility to Society." ACMC *Newsletter* 3, no. 4 (August 1970): 2–11.
– Review of *Socialized Health Services: A Plan for Canada*, edited by Morden Lazarus. *Canadian Welfare* (January–February 1977)
– "Reflections." In *Norman Bethune: His Times and His Legacy*,

edited by David A.E. Shephard and Andrée Lévesque, 229. Ottawa: Canadian Public Health Association 1982.

JOINT PUBLICATIONS

Akhtar, Shahid, and J.W. Macleod. "The Significance of the Chinese Experience in Health Care. In *Health Care in the People's Republic of China: A Bibliography with Abstracts*, by Shahid Akhtar, Ottawa: IDRC 1975.

Badgley, R.F., B.A. Hetherington, and J.W. Macleod. "Social Characteristics and Prediction of Academic Performance of Saskatchewan Medical Students." CMAJ 86 (April 1962): 624.

Elman, R., and J.W. Macleod. "Studies on the Neutralization of Gastric Acidity." *American Journal of Digestive Diseases and Nutrition* 2 (March 1935): 21–6.

Mackenzie, W.C., J.W. Macleod, and J.L Bouchard. "Transpyloric Prolapse of Redundant Gastric Mucosa Folds." CMAJ 54 (1946): 553–8.

Macleod, J.W., et al. "The Management of Peptic Ulcer." Report on round table conference, CMA meeting, Winnipeg. *Manitoba Medical Review* 27 (August 1947).

Macleod, J.W., and D.L. Kippen. "Functional Gastro-intestinal Disorders." *Proceedings of the Royal College of Physicians and Surgeons*, 53–6 (26 November 1948).

Macleod, J.W., and J.S. Thompson. "The Changing Scene in Canadian Medical Education." *Journal of Medical Education* 36, no. 9 (September 1961).

Macleod, J.W., Libbie Park, and Stanley Ryerson. *Bethune: The Montreal Years, An Informal Portrait*. Toronto: James Lorimer 1978.

Meakins, J.C., and J.W. Macleod. "Carcinoma of the Bronchi." CMAJ 28 (1933): 268–75.

Truman, K.R., J.W. Macleod, and D.L. Kippen. "Vagotomy in Duodenal Ulcer." *Manitoba Medical Review* 31, January 1951.

Notes

CHAPTER ONE

1 JWM, biographical note, National Archives of Canada, MG-31, series J30, vol. 13, 12ff.

2 R.B. Macleod, *The Macleod Symposium, June 2–3, 1978*, edited by David Krech (Ithaca, N.Y.: Cornell University, Department of Psychology, 1978).

3 JWM, biographical note.

4 JWM, diary, 1924.

5 JWM, letter to Kenneth Macleod, 18 June 1925.

6 JWM, letter to Helena Brodie Macleod, 21 June 1925.

7 JWM's report to Frontier College for June 1925.

8 *Frontiers*, no. 1 for 1980.

9 JWM, diary, 1924.

10 JWM, biographical note.

11 Ibid.

12 JWM, biographical note.

13 JWM, interview with A.M. Nicholson, Public Archives of Canada, Sound Archives, nos. 8–12, 12 February 1978.

14 Ibid.

15 Ibid.

CHAPTER TWO

1 Interview with Sandy Nicholson, February 1978.

2 Ibid.

3 Richard Allen, *The Social Passion: Religion and Social Reform in Canada, 1914–1928* (Toronto: University of Toronto Press, 1971).

4 Roderick Stewart, *Bethune*. 2nd ed. (Hamden, Conn.: Archon Books, 1973).

5 Interview with Sandy Nicholson.

6 Wendell Macleod, Libbie Park, and Stanley Ryerson, *Bethune: The Montreal Years, An Informal Portrait* (Toronto: James Lorimer, 1978).

7 Interview with Sandy Nicholson.

8 "Reflections on Return from Through the Looking Glass," address delivered to the Montreal Medical Chirurgical Society, 20 December 1935.

9 The details are given in Libbie Park's contribution to *Bethune: The Montreal Years*.

10 Ibid.

11 Ted Allan and Sydney Gordon, *The Scalpel, the Sword* (Montreal: McClelland & Stewart, 1952; revised 1971; reprinted 1981).

CHAPTER THREE

1 JWM, diary, 14 February 1991.

2 Interview with Sandy Nicholson.

3 JWM diary, 23 May 1942.

4 Ibid., 25 May 1942.

5 Ibid., 30 May 1942.

6 Ibid., 8 June 1942.

7 Ibid., 9 June 1942.

8 Ibid., 16 July 1942.

9 Ibid., 15 October 1942.

10 Ibid., 14 November 1942.

11 Ibid.

12 Ibid., 8 April 1943.

13 Ibid., 17 April 1943.

14 Ibid., 21 May 1943.

15 Ibid., 2 September 1943.

16 Interview with Anne McDonald, n.d.

17 JWM diary, 27 March 1945.

18 Ibid., 7 May 1945.

19 JWM, letter to C.J. Tidmarsh, 6 June 1945.

20 JWM, letter to T. Lebbeter, 14 August 1945.

CHAPTER FOUR

1 JWM, diary, 22 November 1945.

2 Interview with Sandy Nicholson.

3   Letter, F. Mott to JWM, 15 November 1946

4   Letter, F. Mott to JWM, 18 November 1947.

5   JWM, diary, 1 July 1948.

6   JWM, note to himself, 30 January 1949.

7   JWM, diary, 1 December 1948.

8   Ibid., 5 December 1948. Mahler's Symphony #2 in C major is known as the "Resurrection Symphony."

9   Ibid., 21 December 1948.

10 Ibid., 31 December 1948.

11 Ibid., 19 May 1949.

12 Ibid., 31 December 1949.

13 Ibid., 14 May 1950.

14 Ibid., 17 May 1950.

15 Ibid., 24 October 1950.

16 Ibid., 17 November 1950.

17 JWM, diary, Jan. 10, 1951.

18 Ibid.

19 Interview with Sandy Nicholson.

20 JWM, diary, 26 January 1951.

21 S. Lindsay to JWM, 3 April 1951, University of Saskatchewan Archives.

22 S. Lindsay to C.J. Mackenzie, 14 April 1951, University Archives.

23 C.J. Mackenzie to S. Lindsay, 19 April 1951, University Archives.

24 S. Lindsay to C.J. Mackenzie.

25 Wilder Penfield to W.P. Thompson, 4 April 1951, University Archives.

26 C.B. Stewart to S. Lindsay, 8 May 1951, University Archives.

27 Alex Richman, letter to Anne McDonald undated.

28 Allan, Klass, letter to Anne McDonald undated.

CHAPTER FIVE

1   A detailed account of the Sigerist committee's findings can be found in L. Horlick's *They Built Better Than They Knew: Saskatchewan's Royal University Hospital, A History, 1955–1992* (University of Saskatchewan Printing Service).

2   F.D. Mott to W.P. Thompson (personal and confidential), 10 November 1950, University Archives.

3   JWM diary, 30 January–20 March 1952.

4   Ibid., 25 March 1952.

5   JWM, "Memorandum to the President for Members of the Board of Governors, University of Saskatchewan, re: Discussion of the College of Medicine," June 24, 1952.

6 "Medical Schools and the Changing Times." A review of a book of that title by Peter V. Lee appears in the *Milbank Memorial Quarterly* 42, no. 1 (January 1964).

7 JWM, diary, 2 January 1953.

8 JWM to D.M. Baltzan, 7 September 1954, University Archives.

9 "Brief to the Education Committee of the College of Physicians and Surgeons of Saskatchewan," 8 October 1954.

10 JWM's response to the Education Committee of the College of Physicians and Surgeons, 8 October 1954, University Archives.

11 The details of the protracted struggle between Macleod and the local practitioners can be found in Horlick's *They Built Better Than They Knew*.

12 JWM to W.P. Thompson, 4 July 1956. University Archives.

13 WPT to JWM, 11 July 1956.

14 I.M. Hilliard to WPT, 6 May 1955, University Archives.

15 WPT to I.M. Hilliard, 10 May 1955, University Archives.

16 The author is indebted to Richard Rempel, professor of history at McMaster University, for an account of the seminar and the role Macleod played in it.

17 Ibid.

18 JWM, "Report to the President," 1959, University Archives.

19 Alexander Robertson, "Developments in the College of Medicine – in Relation to the Department of Social and Preventive Medicine," 1958, University Archives.

20 Interview with Sandy Nicholson.

21 JWM, memo to WPT: "Visit to Porcupine Plain and Tisdale," 24–25 May 1957. University Archives.

22 Bill Waiser, *Saskatchewan: A New History* (Calgary: Fifth House), 2005.

23 Interview with Sandy Nicholson.

24 JWM to J.W.T. Spinks, 28 June 1960, University Archives.

25 JWM, diary, 3 January 1961.

26 Ibid., 2 February 1961.

27 Ibid., 24 May 1961.

28 Ibid., 12 July 1961.

29 Ibid., 19 August 1961.

30 Ibid., Sept. 25, 1961.

31 Ibid., 30 December 1955.

32 J. Graham, letter to author.

CHAPTER SIX

1 Douglas Waugh, "The ACMC and How It Grew," *Canadian Medical Association Journal*, Special Supplement 48, no. 9 (1993), 5–9.
2 Ibid.
3 Clyde V. Kiser, "The Regime of Alexander Robertson, 1962–1969," *The Milbank Memorial Fund: Its Leaders and its Work* (New York: Milbank, 1975).
4 JWM, diary, 1964.
5 *Medical Education in Canada: The MacFarlane Committee Report to the Hall Commission on Health Care.*
6 Ibid.
7 Ibid.
8 JWM, diary, 19 June 1964.
9 Ibid., 24 June 1964.
10 Ibid., 2 January 1964.
11 Sheila Duff Waugh, letter to Louis Horlick, 10 February 2004.
12 Ibid.
13 JWM, diary, 27 February 1970.
14 Sheila Duff Waugh, letter to Louis Horlick, 10 February 2004.
15 W.C. MacKenzie, ACMC *Newsletter* 3, no. 4 (August 1970).
16 ACMC *Newsletter* 3, no. 4 (August 1970).
17 J.F. McCreary, *Canadian Journal of Public Health* 55 (1964) 424.
18 J. Bryant, *Health and the Developing World* (Ithaca, N.Y.: Cornell University Press, 1969), 63.

CHAPTER SEVEN

1 Clyde V. Kiser, *The Milbank Memorial Fund: Its Leaders and Its Work* (New York: Milbank, 1975).
2 *The Milbank Faculty Fellows, 1964–1971* (New York: Milbank, 1968).
3 JWM, diary, 17 September 1963.
4 Interview with Sandy Nicholson.
5 JWM, diary, 18 January 1971.
6 Ibid., 25 May 1971.
7 JWM, letter to Dean Raoul Pierre-Louis, 21 May 1971.
8 JWM, diary, 15 September 1971.
9 Ibid., 17 September 1971.

10 Ibid., 13 December 1971.
11 JWM, letter to Dr Gilles Cormier.
12 JWM, diary, 7 February 1972.
13 Interview with Sandy Nicholson.

CHAPTER EIGHT

1 JWM, letter to Dr Anne Crichton, Community Health Centre Project, Toronto, 3 May 1972.
2 Ibid., 27 March 1972.
3 JWM, diary, 26 January 1975.
4 Betty Bergin, email to author, recollections of Macleod, 5 April 2006.
5 JWM, diary, 13 July 1975.
6 Ibid., 13 October 1976.
7 Ibid., 17 October 1976.
8 Ibid., 18 January 1977.
9 "China Revisited," University of Saskatchewan Archives.
10 Ibid., 26 March 1984.
11 Ibid., 19 August 1984.
12 Ibid., 14 September 1984.
13 Ibid., 30 October 1985.
14 Ibid., 27 April 1985.
15 Lewis Perinbam, WUSC Seminar, 1958.
16 JWM, extract from a letter of appreciation to "a variety of friends," 23 September 1985.
17 JWM, diary, 9 February 1987.
18 Ibid., 8 March 1987.
19 G. Jaworski, email to L. Horlick, 4 January 2005.
20 JWM, letter to H. Barkun, 14 June 1993.
21 Interview with Peter Macleod, 26 May 2004.
22 Jola Sise, letter to L. Horlick, 10 August 2004.
23 Ibid.

CHAPTER NINE

1 Interview with Sandy Nicholson.
2 JWM, introduction of Rod Stewart at a meeting of the Osler Society, McGill University, 1974. The quotation is from Mao Tse Tung's "In Memory of Norman Bethune," *Selected Works*, vol. 2 (New York: International Publishers, 1954), 337–8.
3 JWM, diary, 31 December 1973.

4 JWM, diary, 6 September 1973.

5 Author's interview with Jola Sise, June 2004.

6 JWM, diary, 26 January 1974.

7 JWM, introduction of Rod Stewart at a meeting of the Osler Society, McGill University, 1974.

8 Ibid.

9 JWM, diary, 14 November 1975.

10 Ibid., 9 February 1977.

11 Ibid., 12 March 1977.

12 Ibid., 2 February 1978.

13 Ibid., 13 March 1978.

14 Ibid., 15 June 1978.

15 Ibid., 20 July 1978.

16 "China Revisited: August-September, 1978," lecture given at the Manitoba Health Sciences Centre, 25 January 1979.

17 JWM, diary, 15 July 1979.

18 Ibid., 2 August 1979.

19 Ibid., 2 October 1979.

20 Ibid., 17 November 1979.

21 Ibid., 16 July 1981.

22 Ibid., 18 January 1982.

23 Ibid., 4 April 1982.

24 Ibid., 15 April 1982.

25 Ibid., 6 May 1982.

26 Ibid.

27 JWM, diary, 20 May 1982.

28 Ted Allan, "With Norman Bethune in Spain," in *Norman Bethune: His Times and His Legacy*, 157.

29 Maurice McGregor, "The Bethune Legend: Norman Bethune as Hero," in *Norman Bethune: His Times and His Legacy*, ed. David A.E. Shephard and Andrée Lévesque (Ottawa: Canadian Public Health Association, 1982), 201.

30 JWM, "Reflections," in "Beyond Bethune: Controversy in Today's Health Care – The Quebec Experience," in *Norman Bethune: His Times and His Legacy*, 229.

31 JWM, letter to Vivian Schwartz, 28 May 1983.

32 Alan Hustak, "Co-worker Remembers Bethune," *Montreal Gazette*, Sunday, 23 July 1989.

33 Ruth Wisse, "Dr. Norman Bethune Was More of a Misguided Hero," *Montreal Gazette*, Sunday, 30 July 1989.

34 JWM, letter to Helen Mussallem, 5 September 1989.

CHAPTER TEN

1 JWM, diary, 19 February 1965.
2 Quoted in André Picard, *Critical Care: Canadian Nurses Speak for Change* (Toronto: Harper Collins, 2000).
3 Ibid., April 1966.
4 Ibid., 12 March 1967.
5 Ibid., 9 April 1967.
6 Ibid., 27 April 1967.
7 Ibid., 21 May 1967.
8 Ibid., 24 June 1967.
9 Ibid., June 1967.
10 Ibid., 16 May 1968.
11 Ibid., 3 July 1968.
12 Ibid., 16 December 1968.
13 Ibid., 6 February 1971.
14 Ibid., 28 September 1971.
15 Ibid., 16 November 1971.
16 Ibid., 9 May 1972.
17 Ibid., 15 May 1972.
18 Ibid., 8 October 1972.
19 Ibid., 8 July 1974.
20 Ibid.
21 Ibid., 16 October 1974.
22 Ibid., 11 February 1975.
23 Ibid., 9 March 1975.
24 Ibid., 5 March 1980.
25 Ibid, 31 March 1985.
26 Interview with Jola Sise, 1 June 2004.

CHAPTER ELEVEN

1 JWM, diary, 19 February 1974.
2 Ibid., 14 March 1974.
3 Jola Sise, letter to JWM, 13 March 1974.
4 JWM, letter to Jola Sise (undated).
5 JWM, diary, 27 April 1974.
6 JWM, letter to Jola Sise, 4 May 1974.

7 JWM, diary, 17 June 1974.

8 Jola Sise, letter to L. Horlick, 9 August 2004.

9 Interview with Jola Sise, 1 June 2004.

10 JWM diary, 18 November 1976.

11 Jola Sise, letter to JWM, 14 October 1975.

12 JWM, diary, 18 January 1978.

13 Ibid., 5 March 1980.

14 Ibid., 9 March 1980.

15 Jola Sise, letter to L. Horlick.

16 Ibid.

17 JWM, diary, 19 June 1993.

18 JWM, letter to L. and R. Horlick, July 1996.

19 Interview with Jola Sise, 1 June 2004.

Index